Women Against the Good War

Women

Against the Good War

Conscientious Objection

and Gender on the American

Home Front, 1941–1947

Rachel Waltner Goossen

The University of North Carolina Press

Chapel Hill and London

© 1997

The University of North Carolina Press

All rights reserved

Manufactured in the United States of America

The paper in this book meets the guidelines for permanence
and durability of the Committee on Production Guidelines for
Book Longevity of the Council on Library Resources.

Library of Congress Cataloging-in-Publication Data

Goossen, Rachel Waltner.

Women against the Good War : conscientious objection and gender
on the American home front, 1941–1947 / by Rachel Waltner
Goossen.

p.   cm. — (Gender & American culture)

Includes bibliographical references (p.   ) and index.

ISBN 0-8078-2366-x (cloth: alk. paper). —

ISBN 0-8078-4672-4 (pbk.: alk. paper)

1. World War, 1939–1945 — Conscientious objectors — United
States.   2. World War, 1939–1945 — Moral and ethical aspects.
3. World War, 1939–1945 — Women — United States.   4. Women —
United States — History — 20th century.   I. Title.   II. Series.

D810.C82G66   1997

940.53′162 — dc21   97-9885

                              CIP

01   00   99   98   97   5   4   3   2   1

Portions of this work appeared previously in Rachel Waltner
Goossen, "The 'Second Sex' and the 'Second Milers': Mennonite
Women and Civilian Public Service," *Mennonite Quarterly Review* 66
(October 1992): 525–38.

FOR MY PARENTS

Contents

Illustrations and Tables

TABLES

Acknowledgments

I am grateful to have lived in three communities during the writing of this book and for the assistance of friends and family at each place. In Lawrence, Kansas, historian Ray Hiner was a generous advocate and source of ideas as I began to research this little-known subject in World War II cultural history. Bill Tuttle and Ann Schofield also gave encouragement and guidance for this project from the beginning. An Alfred M. Landon Grant from the Kansas State Historical Society and a University of Kansas fellowship provided crucial early support for research and travel.

My hometown of Goessel, Kansas, population 550 and a three-hour drive from my university base, was a very good — indeed, central — location to be writing about people who had been in Civilian Public Service during World War II because the community and its environs are home to many alumni of that program. Ten miles down the road from Goessel is Bethel College, where the Showalter Oral History Collection on conscientious objectors in World War II is located. On the Bethel campus, historians Keith Sprunger and James Juhnke offered advice on oral history research methods. John Thiesen, Rosemary Moyer, and Greta Hiebert of the Bethel staff located archival documents, photographs, and interlibrary loan materials. Also in central Kansas, longtime friend and mentor Robert Kreider, himself an alumnus of Civilian Public Service, first introduced me to the subject and then over a period of several years helped to identify women and men whose experiences could enrich this book.

In northern Indiana, where I now live, Goshen College has provided two faculty research grants and a congenial setting in which to write and teach. History students Angela Showalter and Ryan Osborne offered welcome assistance as this book neared completion. Thanks also to Goshen colleagues John D. Roth, Marilyn Bayak, Dennis Stoesz, and Joe Springer.

Unforgettable people came to my attention as subjects for this book; it was my good fortune to get to know some of them and to be a guest in their homes. Thanks especially to Lois Kreider, Elizabeth Goering, Naomi Fast, and Nancy and Louis Neumann, as well as to all who shared scrapbooks, correspondence, and the photographs that illustrate this work. For access to other primary source materials I am indebted to Wendy Chmielewski of the Swarthmore College Peace Collection in Swarthmore, Pennsylvania, Hazel Peters of On Earth Peace in New Windsor, Maryland, Lois Bowman of Eastern Mennonite University in Harrisonburg, Virginia, and Kenneth Shaffer of the Brethren Historical Library and Archives in Elgin, Illinois.

Historians in and beyond my geographic communities have contributed in countless ways. I appreciate the words of counsel and critique from Linda Kerber, Ted Wilson, Norman Saul, Paul Boyer, David Smith, Harriet Hyman Alonso, John Oyer, and Theron Schlabach. Working with Kate Torrey and her staff at the University of North Carolina Press has been a pleasure.

My husband, Duane, has been deeply supportive, and our young children, Ben and Elsa, have offered unconditional love and much merriment during the years that this book has been in the making. *Women Against the Good War* is in part about families, and I've often been reminded of mine while mentally immersing myself in the lives of 1940s-era American women. My parents, Lenore and James Waltner, are my bridge to that earlier generation, and I dedicate this book to them with thanks.

Abbreviations

AFSC	American Friends Service Committee
BSC	Brethren Service Committee
CCC	Civilian Conservation Corps
COG	"C.O. Girl"
CPS	Civilian Public Service
FBI	Federal Bureau of Investigation
MCC	Mennonite Central Committee
MNA	Mennonite Nurses' Association
NSBRO	National Service Board for Religious Objectors
PAF	Pacifist Action Fellowship
USO	United Services Organization
WAC	Women's Army Corps
WAVES	Women Accepted for Volunteer Emergency Service
WILPF	Women's International League for Peace and Freedom
WMC	War Manpower Commission
WRL	War Resisters League

Introduction

In the 1990s U.S. citizens give little thought to conscription, the compulsory drafting of civilians into military service. The Americans who served in the Gulf War were enlisted and career personnel, unlike millions of drafted American soldiers who served before them in the Civil War, the two world wars, and in Korea and Vietnam. The recent shift away from conscription is a function of both technology and post–Cold War diplomacy: "smart bombs" and international suasion do not depend on mass mobilization of labor. To be sure, Americans continue to harbor fears about the potential for war. But we breathe more easily than did previous generations on the question of whether national leaders will "send our boys to war." At present, enactment of mass conscription is so unlikely that we have almost no collective memory of the anxieties it created for citizens a half century ago.[1]   VIETNAM

During the Second World War the Selective Training and Service Act of 1940 dictated the terms by which more than thirty-four million American men, ages eighteen to forty-four, participated in the war effort. Because American women remained exempt from draft legislation, they faced choices that differed from those of their husbands, brothers, and sons. Most stayed on the home front but were deeply affected by the absence of male family members and friends. Many entered the labor force, responding to government campaigns that mobilized workers to meet war production demands. Others volunteered for Red Cross work and entered service-oriented vocations. Still others ran households efficiently in spite of wartime shortages and assumed responsibilities on farms and in family businesses that, except for the war, would have been shouldered by men.

A small minority of Americans were pacifists, even in this most popular of wars. In recent years it has often been called the "good war," a term linked to Studs Terkel's 1984 acclaimed book of that name. Yet during the war one hundred thousand men in the United States — including an estimated fifty thousand noncombatants — claimed conscientious objector status.[2] As an alternative to participating in the armed forces, more than six thousand men, 70 percent of them Jehovah's Witnesses, went to prison for refusing to cooperate with Selective Service. Another twelve thousand men entered Civilian Public Service (CPS), a government-sponsored program designed to accommodate conscientious objectors. Three historic peace churches — the Mennonites, Friends, and Brethren — administered Civilian Public Service, which offered the opportunity to do "work of national importance," such as forestry, soil conservation, or mental health work.

A unique wartime program, CPS has been documented in historical and sociological studies as well as in the memoirs of World War II conscientious objectors.[3] Yet most chroniclers have assumed that Civilian Public Service was exclusively a man's world. To the contrary, approximately two thousand women, and perhaps half as many children, lived in and near Civilian Public Service camps.[4] The majority of these families, though by no means all, had ties with Christian pacifist groups.

The term "pacifism," defined as opposition to participating in war, appears more frequently in postwar vocabularies than in the language of World War II conscientious objectors. One CPS alumnus suggests that scholars find the term useful "because it serves as a modifier, a noun, and an ideology."[5] But during the 1940s the Amish, as well as some conservative Mennonite and Brethren groups, rejected it as too secular, too politically motivated. They favored instead the concept of "nonresistance," derived from a New Testament ethic (Jesus' admonition, "Do not resist one who is evil").[6] At the same time, other C.O.s — including some who were nonreligious and others who vehemently resisted conscription but did not necessarily oppose the war — also spurned the pacifist label. Despite their many ideological disagreements, however, men in Civilian Public Service generally accepted the term "C.O."

Women who opposed the war were not in any legal sense conscientious objectors, for despite a looming threat that American women might be drafted to ease military "manpower" needs, they never actually faced conscription. Yet during World War II many more citizens — men and women — identified themselves as conscientious objectors than actually obtained that status from local draft boards. Because of their gender, pacifist women had little chance to declare their sentiments publicly. Elise Boulding, the noted sociologist and peace scholar, told a biographer: "I remember feeling, like many women did, that I wished I were a man so that my conscientious objection could be recorded."[7]

This book focuses on home front women who thought of themselves as C.O.s, especially those who became part of Civilian Public Service. On the strength of their beliefs, these women distanced themselves from the most momentous event of their generation.

Cultures of Nonconformity

Scholars interested in the experiences of women workers during World War II have compiled a rich historiography. Two decades ago, William Chafe concluded that the accelerated entry of American women into the labor force signified a "watershed" in their history. More recently, however, historians have argued that women's work outside the home during wartime fit well with Americans' conventional notions of women as helpmates.[8] Anthropologist Micaela di Leonardo rightly contends that these scholars have "challenged the image of war-fueled feminist advances by documenting workplace discrimination and exploitation, increased public harassment, and the exploitative uses of feminine symbols for military purposes."[9]

At the same time that historians have been producing empirical studies, social scientists, literary critics, and others have been constructing theoretical works on war, peace, and gender. These scholars have been reluctant to catalogue and assess the "impact" of war on women. Jean Bethke Elshtain, for example, recalls the naïveté of her own World War II childhood in which she had the impression that "the woman on the home front just waits." As a girl observing her elders, Elshtain believed that American women had "no story to tell because 'nothing happened,' no life and death conflict" had challenged them.[10] Lynne Hanley points out that a similar perspective dominates the canon of twentieth century war literature. With few exceptions, the "classic" memoirs of American men — famous writers and soldiers, not women or noncombatants — have defined the experience of war.[11]

Increasingly, historians of World War II have turned to oral history to scrutinize men's and women's experiences. In addition to Studs Terkel's landmark work, Cynthia Eller's *Conscientious Objectors and the Second World War* analyzes the process of ethical decision making by male C.O.s. Heather Frazer and John O'Sullivan's *"We Have Just Begun to Not Fight"* offers oral history perspectives from Civilian Public Service assignees.

Sherna Berger Gluck's *Rosie the Riveter Revisited* focuses on forty-five women aircraft workers from southern California, and Amy Kesselman's *Fleeting Opportunities* examines women workers who defied proscribed gender roles while working in American shipyards.[12]

The historiography of American women and World War II thins considerably when one adds the dimension of pacifism. Women who took part in Civilian Public Service were not drafted and therefore received little official or public notice. In subsequent years, few of them published memoirs or spoke publicly about their wartime experiences. Accordingly, scholars of the peace movement and of the American home front have excluded their experiences from historical accounts. Peace scholarship has focused instead on prominent antimilitarists who took a radical stance against the war.[13]

In 1943 Dorothy Day, cofounder of the Catholic Worker movement, decried what she believed to be an insidious campaign enslaving women to "work in the factories throughout the land to make the bombers, the torpedoes, the explosives, the tools of war."[14] Day echoed the sentiments of Jane Addams, who earlier in the century had proposed a "moral substitute for war" and had envisioned a time when women would be coequal, enfranchised citizens engaged in building a peaceful society on the basis of voluntarism rather than coercion.[15] U.S. Congresswoman Jeannette Rankin of Montana, a contemporary of both Addams and Day, was first elected to Congress in 1916; a year later she voted against the United States' entry to war. She lost her seat in Congress during the next campaign but was reelected in 1940 and cast the only vote against the United States' entrance into World War II. Other prominent peace activists include Mildred Scott Olmsted, executive secretary of the U.S. section of the Women's International League for Peace and Freedom (WILPF) from 1935 to 1966, and Dorothy Detzer, who served as WILPF's lobbyist on Capitol Hill during the Second World War.[16]

But lesser-known women whose lives intersected with Civilian Public Service also opposed the war. Their stories are the subject of this book. Like the women a generation before them who questioned the nation's entry into the First World War and those who a generation later resisted the draft during the Vietnam War, women who took part in Civilian Public Service during World War II offered moral and material support to conscripted men who shared their convictions. "Perhaps young women have not been called upon to make their decisions known in as much of a public way," declared a woman who married a C.O. two months before his release from Civilian Public Service in 1946, "but nevertheless many have stood by their brothers, husbands, and friends."[17]

The majority of these women, including those who were Mennonite or Brethren, had grown up in traditions with strong communitarian and patriarchal emphases. In the most conservative of these family and church contexts, women found few openings to discuss their views. One Mennonite woman commented: "My father did not quiz prospective daughters-in-law on their attitudes to pacifism."[18] Mennonite and Brethren family dynamics varied widely, but women were generally not expected to involve themselves in public affairs.

Other pacifist families, particularly those belonging to the Society of Friends, held more liberal views on the freedom of the individual to choose, as well as on gender equality. Margaret Taylor Kurtz, born and reared in Pennsylvania, described her background:

> I was raised in a close family — grandparents were all Quakers. I heard many Bible stories from the Old and New Testaments. My father frequently quoted bits such as 'and the greatest of these is love,' or 'perfect love casteth out all fear.' He had been a C.O. with farm deferment in World War I, my brother the same in World War II. An older sister went to Egypt with the United Nations Relief agency as a lab technician. Another sister's husband refused to register and went to prison for eighteen months in Danbury, Connecticut.[19]

Kurtz, whose career as a nurse began during the Second World War, contacted the American Friends Service Committee with the hope of finding an alternative to military nursing. In 1944 she accepted an assignment in Trenton, North Dakota, as a CPS nurse.

Still other women were raised in families that were divided in their attitudes toward war. Margaret Calbeck Neal, raised in a Methodist family, remembered that her father, a World War I vet, "did not join the American Legion or wear his uniform after coming home. He told stories about the French and German people and culture but never about the war itself. He always displayed a large flag on national holidays. But during World War II when my brothers were in the army in China and Europe and my mother complained, 'I didn't raise my boys to kill or be killed,' his only response was: 'The army will make *men* out of them!' "[20]

Other young American women observed similar disagreements at home. Joyce Lancaster Wilson characterized her father as a "patriotic war-supporter" and her mother as "an intense pacifist and Christian

Scientist"; the couple divorced in the early 1920s, when Joyce was ten. Strongly antiwar by 1932, the year she entered Barnard College, Wilson attributed her views to her mother's conviction and to her own extensive reading of literature and philosophy.[21] Elizabeth Doe Jaderborg, the daughter of an American Baptist minister, recalled that in the 1940s her C.O. leanings put her at odds with her brother in the Air Corps. But after the war, Jaderborg learned that their family background included "Quakers who suffered in Plymouth and followed Roger Williams to Rhode Island. There were Loyalists, too, and many who sought peace and quiet in Nova Scotia during the Revolution."[22]

Lillian Doucette of Rochester, New York, shared in her husband Louis's struggle to obtain C.O. status. A Catholic, Louis Doucette appealed to federal authorities, including President Roosevelt, after being denied conscientious objector status by his local draft board. In 1942 he was assigned the C.O. classification IV-E, which meant that he was eligible for Civilian Public Service. Before the Doucettes's marriage in 1941, Lillian had become a committed pacifist through the influence of a high school teacher and several ministers. Later she recalled: "My parents, both British, were pro-war. Both of my brothers were in the service. We had many discussions, and there was much pressure for me to change my thinking. However, when my mother was interviewed by the F.B.I., she did say that she thought my Louis was sincere and that he had, for as long as she'd known him, stated his pacifist views."[23]

Most of the women who became involved with Civilian Public Service were steeped in the teachings of the historic peace churches — the Mennonites, Brethren, and Friends. They enjoyed the support of their families and church communities. Often the people they knew best — parents, siblings, relatives, friends, and even high school and college teachers — shared and reinforced their perspectives on pacifism, race relations, and other contemporary issues. These cultures of nonconformity, though hardly visible to most Americans, shaped the childhood and adolescent years of women who reached young adulthood during the Second World War.

Doris Cline Egge, reared in a Church of the Brethren community near Harrisonburg, Virginia, recalled that in 1940 her church youth group assembled to talk about the likelihood that the United States would be drawn into the war. Adult church leaders explained that boys near the age of eighteen could expect to be drafted, and that girls, too, should prepare for the possibility of conscription:

So we role-played draft boards, with the adults really interrogating girls and boys in the youth group about what we were going to do. And we girls were [expected] to claim a position just like the men were.

It had such an impact on my life, that it carried me through a very bad experience. My best friend's brothers all went into the service and her father used to take me on when I was visiting, and say, 'How does it feel to have a brother with a yellow streak up his back,' and those kinds of things.

And the influence of the youth group leaders was so strong that I remember being in college and being semi-engaged, and then pulling back from that, because he went into the Navy. I felt like I *was* a conscientious objector . . . because of the influences of my life.[24]

This description of girlhood preparations for conscription illustrates both the nonconformist tendencies of the historic peace churches and their penchant for corporate witness. My effort to uncover the stories of C.O. women has been eased by my own identity as a Mennonite and because my background bears some resemblance to theirs. Born in 1960 to a Mennonite pastor and homemaker, I grew up with family lore that included references to my great-uncle, Edward J. B. Waltner, a South Dakota farmer who was a conscientious objector during the First World War. After ten months in various military camps, Uncle Ed was assigned to work at a veterinary hospital at Camp Cody, New Mexico, where he refused to follow a command from a military officer to "drill, take care of sick animals, and obey all orders."[25] He was court-martialed, and from May 1918 to January 1919 served a prison term at Fort Leavenworth with about 350 other religious objectors. On the day he was released, his wife of twenty-one months, Anna, waited impatiently "on the street before the prison entrance early before sunrise."[26] Less remote to me as a child was the war in Vietnam, which my parents fervently opposed. Ours was a family that supported presidential candidates with antiwar views: Eugene McCarthy in 1968, George McGovern in 1972.

By 1980 I was a student at Bethel College, a Mennonite-affiliated liberal arts college in central Kansas. That year, President Jimmy Carter, responding to the Soviet Union's invasion of Afghanistan, revived the requirement of draft registration for eighteen-year-old men. This change in policy generated significant antidraft activism. More than 350 student and peace groups around the country staged rallies on college campuses and picket lines at post offices, as well as sit-ins at congressional offices and federal buildings. From New York to San Francisco demonstrators urged young men to seek draft counseling before registering. Echoing the massive campus protests of the Vietnam era, some students engaged in civil disobedience and were arrested. From 1980 to 1984, approximately half a million young men refused to register, nearly twice as many as had refused during the Vietnam years, 1964 to 1973.[27]

At the Bethel campus in Kansas, we women students tried to find ways to support our friends who were considering whether or not they ought to register. Two of my acquaintances who defied Selective Service law went to trial. Just in case women would become subject to draft legislation, some of us filed two-page forms with Mennonite denominational offices detailing our claim for classification as C.O.s. Church leaders advised us to attach to these documents letters of reference from pastors, teachers, or other adults who knew us well.

Looking back, I recognize this experience as a typically Mennonite response to government authority. Historic peace church institutions—including congregations, schools, and extended family networks—lent support to young people struggling with matters of conscience. So it had been four decades earlier, on the eve of World War II, when leaders of the historic peace churches envisioned Civilian Public Service as an alternative for men opposed to participating in war.

Historical Perspectives

This book focuses on the wartime experiences of women who became part of the Civilian Public Service program on the American home front. Primary sources for uncovering the histories of these women include archival evidence, private writings such as letters and diaries, oral history interviews, and questionnaire responses. Oral history interviews with 27 women and the questionnaire responses of 153 women yielded a new data base of 180 who took part in this wartime program of alternative service.[28]

To obtain as broad a sample of informants as possible, I gathered the names and addresses of women attending fiftieth-anniversary CPS reunions and mailed questionnaires to them. (The questionnaire used is reprinted in the appendix.) One beneficial aspect of this method of data gathering was that I was able to inform several hundred women of my interest in gaining access to correspondence, photographs, and other privately held documents. Since these reunions were dominated by Mennonites, I also sent questionnaires to women whose names appeared on Brethren CPS alumni lists and to women who had served in Quaker-led CPS camps. Of the 229 women who received questionnaires about their involvement in Civilian Public Service, 153 women, or 67 percent, responded. This return rate was surprisingly high, considering that the average age of respondents was seventy-two years.

Statistical profiles of respondents appear in Chapters 2 and 3. Sixty-one percent of the women in this sample were Mennonites at the time of World War II. The predominance of Mennonites in this study reflects the leadership exerted by the denomination's service agency, the Mennonite Central Committee (MCC). Although only 39 percent of the men who entered CPS were Mennonite or Amish, MCC worked aggressively throughout the war to keep the program viable and recruited hundreds of women to serve as Civilian Public Service staff. So while the combined sample of 180 women in this study is not representative of all American women pacifists during the war (for example, it does not include women whose C.O. husbands served as noncombatants in the military), it *does* provide an aggregate snapshot of the women who took part in Civilian Public Service.[29]

Most of these respondents profess solid antiwar commitments and retain connections to a network of World War II conscientious objectors. They have survived five decades beyond young adulthood and rely on fallible memories in recounting events from the 1940s. Their willingness to provide information suggests that they value highly their participation in Civilian Public Service. Whenever possible, I have tried to corroborate their memories with documentation originating in the 1940s. But because this study focuses on persons who were never drafted, documentary evidence is scarce.[30]

Chapter 1 of this book examines the federal government's conscription policies and provides an orientation to the program of Civilian Public Service. Chapter 2 describes the cultural milieu of the American home front from the perspectives of women and men dissenters. Chapter 3 explores the lives of Civilian Public Service "camp followers," women who crisscrossed the country to live and work near their husbands, fiancés, and friends. Since Selective Service provided no support to the dependents of conscientious objectors — in contrast to the support given military families — many of these women negotiated a precarious place in American society, burdened by financial worries, family disruptions, and hostility from local communities. Chapter 4 surveys the experiences of professionally educated dietitians and nurses who staffed the 151 CPS camps and units spanning the U.S. mainland, the Virgin Islands, and Puerto Rico. Chapter 5 focuses on idealistic college-age women who called themselves "C.O. Girls" or "CPS women" and who took part in short-term assignments as psychiatric aides in state mental hospitals. At these institutions, administrators welcomed them as badly needed replacements for employees who had been drafted or who had left for better-paying jobs. And finally, Chapter 6 examines the impact of demobilization and assesses the meaning of Civilian Public Service for women in the postwar years.

Women who identified themselves as conscientious objectors shared many of the cultural ideals of their generation. Most were determined to offer moral support to drafted men who were entering Civilian Public Service, beginning prison sentences, or choosing noncombatant roles in the military. These women's work often reinforced traditional gender roles. In that respect, their stories conform closely to the patterns of limited opportunity for women on the American home front.

And yet, this book offers a new perspective on American women in wartime. The analysis of gender within a marginalized population — conscientious objectors — reveals alternative behavior on the home front. These women made unusual choices, questioned government dictums, and defied societal expectations, all of which set them apart from the millions of Americans who supported the war effort. By walking against a powerful stream, women C.O.s learned lessons of nonconformity that sustain them still. Although more than half a century has passed, the experiences of these conscientious objectors are indeed relevant to present-day debates about the status of women and men in a democratic, militarized society.

1 The Conscripting of Civilians

The story of Civilian Public Service veers from the broader history and popular culture of the American home front. Citizens who opposed the war on religious or philosophical grounds found themselves isolated from the vast majority of Americans. Yet they too claimed the moral high ground. Like Americans who supported the war with heart, mind, and soul, many who opposed it invoked pietistic language. In March 1941 a C.O. college student published an essay declaring his eagerness for alternative service: "We, who will go to camp, should . . . make of it a blessing for God, for mankind, and for ourselves. Perhaps there we will see the truth that this is a God-centered and not a man-centered world."[1]

During World War II American pacifists came to no consensus on where to draw the line for war-related work. Each of the historic peace churches had some members who entered military service as noncombatants and others who accepted regular I-A classification for combatant duty.[2] But despite the war's immense popularity, tens of thousands of American men eligible for the draft identified themselves as conscientious objectors. Casting a critical eye on the war, they looked for ways to avoid participation. Some sought deferment for health reasons or because they were engaged in farming or ministerial work. Others, who chose Civilian Public Service or went to prison, thought long and hard about the war and their relation to it. Some conscientious objectors did not consider themselves pacifists but objected to the war on political grounds. Most objectors, however, did embrace pacifism and offered wide-ranging justifications for it.

For many persons raised in the historic peace church denominations, the combination of family history and deeply rooted religious ideology produced staunch pacifist convictions, even in the face of mass mobilization. Anna Wiebe Miller, a Mennonite who volunteered as a music educator in Civilian Public Service camps, noted that her father had immigrated as a young man to the United States to avoid being drafted into the Russian army. As his children grew he regaled them with stories of the terror experienced by Russian Mennonites, whose prosperous agricultural settlements and industries on the steppes of the Ukraine had been destroyed during the revolution. The theme in these accounts of people struggling to retain their heritage of nonresistance impressed upon Anna that pacifism was an essential element of the family's religious tradition, stretching back four centuries to the Anabaptist movement of sixteenth-century Europe.[3]

Like the Wiebes, families who were Mennonite, Brethren, and Quaker drew on rich oral and written traditions of peace activism from the time of the Reformation to the First World War. These religious groups expected members to live out a firmly held set of beliefs, including nonparticipation in war, that went against the grain of the broader culture. One result was that these religious objectors drew sustenance from their unique tradition but did not necessarily engage deeply in political analysis of any particular war — even the spread of fascism in Europe in the 1930s and early 1940s. For most religious pacifists, the essential question was not whether a nation's military action was justifiable. They rejected state-sanctioned violence and believed that they could not conscientiously participate in it. As citizens in a country mobilizing for war, they focused on finding alternatives to military service and offering humanitarian aid to suffering people abroad.

Religious scholar Cynthia Eller, in examining the moral reasoning of World War II C.O.s, found that some believed that the war was necessary yet refused to participate as combatants because they were Christians. Others, who were much more critical of the state, viewed the war as "based on greed and self-righteousness. They carefully pointed out the ways in which the United States aided and abetted Hitler, how the Allies added to the rising level of hostilities between themselves and the Axis powers, and how very many people were killed or left homeless by a war whose root conflicts could have been solved in more peaceful ways."[4] Margaret Calbeck Neal, a longtime peace activist and a friend during

World War II to many Civilian Public Service assignees, reflected this perspective years later. Asked about the phrase "the good war," Neal responded: "At the time, everyone except my pacifist friends seemed to be in favor of the war. We now know that our government's reasons for entering it were not as idealistic as then claimed. If we really cared about Hitler's oppression of the Jews, why did we refuse to admit that boatload of refugees?"[5]

The plight of European Jews, made apparent to American observers in June 1939 when the *St. Louis* tried unsuccessfully to dock on American shores, was a profound concern of some conscientious objectors. Both Christian pacifist organizations such as the American Friends Service Committee and secular ones like the U.S. section of the Women's International League for Peace and Freedom lobbied the Roosevelt administration to admit Jewish refugees. But even after a heightening of public concern, Congress rejected efforts to amend immigration restrictions.[6]

During the war most American C.O.s, despite their humanitarian impulses, knew little of the mass murders underway in Europe. Ruth Niesley Zercher, the wife of a CPS assignee, worked alongside her husband and other C.O.s as a mental health aide at a hospital in Howard, Rhode Island. Among her contacts were Jewish residents and a Jewish doctor, all recent immigrants from eastern Europe. Zercher remembers her utter surprise when the doctor chastised her for calling a patient by her first name and ordered her to address the woman as "Mrs." A coworker explained to Zercher that the doctor's insistence on formality and respect on the ward derived from his outrage at Nazi injustices and at American anti-Semitism. For Zercher, who at the time knew almost nothing of the situation of European Jews, the doctor's passion for dignity had a profound impact.[7]

Few women or men in Civilian Public Service could claim any real understanding of Jewish perspectives. Most C.O.s assigned to the program were unlikely to rub shoulders with American Jews who might have tried to raise their consciousness. Of the more than twelve thousand men who entered the program, only 60 identified themselves as Jewish.[8] After the war ended in Europe and concentration camp survivors were freed, American conscientious objectors were among those most surprised and dismayed at their revelations.

Had they known about the European "final solution," some American conscientious objectors likely would have joined the war effort. But in reality few abandoned their peace convictions. The great majority of C.O.s, despite concerns about the evil represented by Hitler, remained firmly committed to pacifist ideology.[9]

Gender and Wartime Experience

On the eve of World War II, the historic peace churches were well-established religious subcultures of nonconformity on the larger American landscape. What happened to their members who were drafted in wartime — a cohort of white men mostly in their early and middle twenties, mostly unmarried, one third of them farmers or farm laborers, many without college backgrounds — is a study of the paradox of social change. In opting for a C.O. stance, many male draftees faced ridicule and derision from Americans who did not understand or respect their position. But the emasculating climate in which American C.O.s found themselves, teeming with hyped-up 1940s patriotism, does not adequately convey their collective experience. For against this larger cultural backdrop, the Civilian Public Service program offered C.O.s opportunities for geographic mobility, education, and vocational training; and many CPS assignees found that these new experiences outweighed the negative implications of their stance.

How did women who took part in Civilian Public Service fare? Did they feel peripheral, believing that their sacrifice was less than that of the men they joined? Did they resent the inequities of a wartime culture that recognized men as military heroes — or even as conscientious objectors willing to serve their country — while giving secondary consideration to women's citizenship obligations?

These questions suggest that American men and women pacifists in the 1940s, at least those who became associated with Civilian Public Service, viewed their experiences through a lens that emphasized gender difference. Yet it is clear that the women who took part in the program did *not* link their activism with concerns for gender equality. Perhaps because so many of them had come of age in families and in church communities with strong patriarchal emphases, they hardly questioned the assumption that Civilian Public Service was a program designed largely by men, and for men. Furthermore, the marginalized status of American pacifists in wartime society prompted many of these women — wives, fiancées, sisters of C.O.s — to function as de facto auxiliaries to the men in their lives. As historian Paul Boyer notes, American women in Civilian Public Service settings "faced ridicule and contempt from other women, for example, in situations where ideology clearly prevailed over gender in determining the dynamics of the interaction."[10] Loyalty to friends and family, combined with ideals of pacifism and compassionate service, motivated women to take part in CPS far more than did notions of sisterhood.

And yet, for women as for men, Civilian Public Service work became a conduit by which they were able to broaden social contacts, travel, and think more deeply about the implications of peace activism. Thus a paradox remains at the center of this story. Many of the people who entered Civilian Public Service from traditions rooted in political detachment and cultural nonconformity would emerge from CPS much more willing to engage the world around them. For the rest of their lives, they would regard this wartime program as a foundation for their interest in a multitude of causes, including antiwar activism, racial justice, and — especially for many women alumni — issues of gender equality.

Conscription and Conscience

Civilian Public Service evolved out of the Selective Training and Service Act of 1940. Compared to its legal precedents, the new law offered generous provisions for conscientious objectors. It succeeded the Selective Service Act of 1917, a measure that during World War I had proven unacceptable to both peace groups and military officials. The earlier law had stated that only men who belonged to "well-recognized" religious groups that opposed participation in war could receive classification as C.O.s. Thus, of the 64,693 Americans who sought C.O. status in World War I, those who did so on socialist or other philosophical grounds, or who lacked ties to the historic peace churches, had no lawful basis for their claims.

During World War I local Selective Service boards granted C.O. status to nearly nine out of every ten men who requested it. But the 1917 law made no satisfactory provision for C.O.s. It provided exemption only from combat, not from other forms of military service. As a result, many of the religious objectors whose claims *were* recognized by the state were coerced into noncombatant service in the medical corps, quartermaster corps, and engineer service.[11] Some draft-age men fled to Canada without registering for the draft, and a few entire Mennonite and Hutterite communities — representing about eighteen hundred men, women, and children — migrated to Canada in response to conscription.[12]

In the politically repressive climate of the First World War, American conscientious objectors were vulnerable to mistreatment and ridicule. World War I C.O.s routinely heard themselves called cowards, parasites, shirkers, or "yellow-bellies." Thousands were inducted into the army. The Wilson administration failed to instruct military officers on how to deal with these men, many of whom did not conform to the routines of training camp. The result was harassment of C.O.s by rank-and-file soldiers and, less commonly, by commanding officers. More than five hundred C.O.s were court-martialed and sent to federal prison. The most extreme cases of punitive treatment occurred at Alcatraz in California and at Camp Funston in Kansas, where some conscientious objectors who refused to wear military uniforms were beaten and denied medical treatment for life-threatening illness. As many as seventeen abused C.O.s lost their lives. Joseph Hofer, a Hutterite who refused to wear a uniform, was locked in a cell and tortured; eventually he contracted pneumonia. In November 1918 he died in a military hospital where, in one last, cruel act, officials dressed his body in a uniform before shipping him back to his family.[13]

Not until 1933, when Franklin D. Roosevelt entered the White House, were the last World War I C.O.s remaining in prison granted full pardon. During the interwar years a loose coalition of religious and secular peace organizations worked to reform federal policies governing conscientious objectors. Cooperation among these groups did not come easily, for they represented perspectives ranging from apoliticism to internationalism. Amish and some conservative Mennonite groups, for example, refrained from participation in the political order — even voting — as an expression of their separation from warfare and other "worldly" endeavors. Yet to be effective in Washington they realized that they would need to build coalitions. In 1935 representatives of three peace churches, Mennonite, Brethren, and Friends, formed a standing committee to explore proposals for wartime alternative service. In 1937 and again in 1940 delegations representing these churches met with President Roosevelt to discuss their proposals.[14]

Through the thirties, pacifist organizations struggled futilely to articulate consistent positions on the United States' neutrality laws and related agenda. Pacifists, though divided on American foreign policy, generally remained critical of populists such as Gerald L. K. Smith or isolationist groups like the National Legion of Mothers of America.[15] Few pacifists were drawn to the antiinterventionism of Charles Lindbergh, whose organization, the America First Committee, lobbied for a strong military defense in response to Nazism. Far more took their cues from the social gospel or from socialist political philosophy. Many Quakers, Mennonites, and Brethren had warmly embraced social gospel teachings that had infused liberal Protestantism in the first half of the twentieth century. This strand in the religious ideology of these churches helps to explain why many of their members could not endorse isolationism. Ilona Hensel, raised in the pacifist Brethren in Christ tradition, reflected years after her involvement in CPS that "I often wondered where would Jesus have been, if in our circumstances, and I felt like he would be on the battlefield ministering to the wounded and dying."[16]

As the nation edged toward Allied participation in war, religious and secular pacifist groups rallied in response to the Burke-Wadsworth bill, a measure proposed to meet national manpower needs. During the summer of 1940 civil liberties, antiwar, and religious organizations led by the American Civil Liberties Union, the War Resisters League, and the American Friends War Problems Committee lobbied against the bill.[17] Aware that American public opinion remained chilly toward their cause and recognizing the long odds against defeating the proposed legislation, these groups directed their efforts at moderating its provisions for conscientious objectors. (A 1940 Gallup poll found that only 13 percent of Americans believed that conscientious objectors should be granted exemption from military service, and 37 percent thought they should be assigned to noncombatant jobs. The remainder of those polled thought that C.O.s should be assigned to regular military service, imprisoned, or receive the death penalty.)[18]

Yet key congressional officials wanted to avoid the kinds of disgraceful incidents that had occurred in 1917–18. They were receptive to the suggestions of religious and pacifist leaders on the issue of conscientious objection, and on September 16, 1940, when President Roosevelt signed the new Selective Training and Service Act, he ensured that government policy toward C.O.s would be considerably more generous than in the First World War. Section 5(g), the new law's provision on conscientious objection, stated that persons who could not participate in war "by reason of religious training and belief" would be exempt from combatant training. For the first time, American men could legitimately claim Catholicism, mainline Protestantism, or other religious influences as the basis of their objection to military service.

Under the new law, drafted men who were conscientiously opposed to noncombatant service would be "assigned to work of national importance under civilian direction."[19] This language represented a victory for groups concerned about protecting the rights of conscientious objectors. Yet the law was vague on the crucial issue of how C.O.s would meet their obligations to the state. During the next half decade the new legislation would open a Pandora's box of church-state tensions over issues of individual liberty. Around the country sixty-five hundred local draft boards would review registrants' applications and determine who was available for induction, who should be classified as conscientious objectors, and who should be deferred.[20]

The framers of the Selective Training and Service Act of 1940 realized that some conscientious objectors would resist the new law. Government and church officials alike hoped that provision 5(g) would result in relatively few objectors going to prison. Yet *more* draftees — including some who were denied C.O. status by their draft boards, others who refused to accept Civilian Public Service assignments, and still others who left CPS illegally — went to prison in World War II than had during World War I. The percentage of men drafted and imprisoned for draft violations from 1940 to 1946 was triple the percentage of C.O.s imprisoned in 1918 and 1919. In all, 6,086 conscientious objectors went to prison during World War II for violating the Selective Training and Service Act.[21]

Not all imprisoned C.O.s were pacifists. More than four thousand were Jehovah's Witnesses who maintained that each member of the sect was a minister. Witnesses took the position that while they would be willing to fight for millenarianist causes, they wanted no part of battles fought on behalf of secular governments. Although conscripted Witnesses sought ministerial exemptions, most local draft boards denied their requests. Even when offered deferment on other grounds or offered assignments in Civilian Public Service, most of the Witnesses refused. Thus, as legal scholar Stephen M. Kohn points out, the normally law-abiding Jehovah's Witnesses who went to prison during World War II did so "not because of anti-war convictions, but because of religious misunderstanding, prejudice, and persecution."[22]

The remainder of imprisoned World War II C.O.s — 1,675 men — came from a cross section of religious and political backgrounds. Most shared a belief in the responsibility of the individual to speak out against war. Psychiatrist Robert M. Lindner, who studied imprisoned World War II conscientious objectors, wrote in 1946 that among this small population he found "true humanitarians. . . . They recognize the moral wrongfulness of war, perceive the skeleton beneath the uniform, reject the sonorous talk of our leaders, and armed with history and statistics seek to convince the rest of us. Yet they . . . undergo considerable torment in the course of their resistance."[23]

Like the twelve thousand objectors who accepted Civilian Public Service assignments, C.O.s in prison sought support from their mothers, wives, and other family members and friends. Julius Eichel, the only American to be imprisoned in both World War I and II for draft resistance, joined his wife Esther in organizing a support group, the Friends and Families of Imprisoned C.O.s. The group met in the Eichels' Brooklyn apartment and later at a Manhattan labor union hall. Attendance at these meetings averaged about twenty; most who came were mothers of prisoners. Members read aloud from their loved ones' letters, and "if the letters contained news of abusive treatment," Esther Eichel later recalled, "the group sent off telegrams to protest to the wardens and other officials."[24] The group also mailed to public officials, prison administrators, and journalists a newsletter edited by Julius Eichel, *The Absolutist*, which publicized antiwar perspectives and promoted amnesty. Four decades later, the noted antiwar activist Dave Dellinger paid tribute to women supporters of imprisoned C.O.s. "In so many cases, like my own wife," he recalled, "they had a less spectacular, more difficult path . . . without being adequately recognized as the brave and often lonely pioneers of a better future that they certainly were."[25]

Some World War II C.O.s served prison terms for as long as five years. Afterward many committed themselves to activism in the War Resisters League and related organizations. Two resisters, poet Robert Lowell and author Carleton Mabee, went on to win Pulitzer prizes; another, Bayard Rustin, became a leader in the civil rights movement. In the postwar period many formerly jailed C.O.s would work with alumni of Civilian Public Service in promoting peace and civil rights causes.[26]

Launching Civilian Public Service

During the fall of 1940 passage of the Selective Training and Service Act cleared the way for leaders of the major peace churches — the Mennonites, Brethren, and Friends — to negotiate with Selective Service officials the contours of a new national civilian service program. Taking the lead in planning CPS were three service agencies, the Mennonite Central Committee (MCC), Brethren Service Committee (BSC), and American Friends Service Committee (AFSC), each a cooperative organization sup-

Staff and C.O.s at the first CPS camp to open, Patapsco, Maryland, May 1941. The three women who lived at Patapsco in the camp's earliest months were Louise Wilson, dietitian Nancy Foster, and nurse Alice Beaman. (*Nancy Neumann, Maineville, Ohio*)

ported by Mennonite, Brethren, and Friends constituencies. Mennonite Central Committee, for example, represented Old Order Amish, Amish Mennonites, Mennonite Brethren, Brethren in Christ, the Mennonite Church, General Conference Mennonites, Holdeman Mennonites, and other groups.[27]

In October these three service organizations established the National Service Board for Religious Objectors (NSBRO), an agency authorized by the federal government to operate Civilian Public Service. Throughout the war NSBRO would function as an intermediary between church agency officials and Selective Service, which would oversee the total program. In addition, it would champion the rights of individual C.O.s, including nonreligious objectors.

During the winter of 1940–41 representatives of the church agencies, Selective Service officials, and President Roosevelt considered various plans for the administration and financing of Civilian Public Service. On February 6, 1941, the president signed an executive order authorizing Selective Service to draw up camp regulations for C.O.s, and within days the church agencies began preparing old Civilian Conservation Corps (CCC) camps in anticipation of the first CPS assignees. The work done at the camps would benefit the soil conservation, forestry, national park,

U.S. Forest Service work performed by conscientious objectors at Royalston, Massachusetts. (*American Friends Service Committee, Civilian Public Service, Swarthmore College Peace Collection, Swarthmore, Pennsylvania*)

and land reclamation bureaus of the federal government. Church leaders expected that Selective Service would approve additional work settings for CPS assignees in coming months. The government agencies agreed to pay for tools and technical supervision for the work done by Civilian Public Service men, while church sponsors planned to cover the camps' education, health, recreation, and maintenance costs. Throughout the war administrative policies would vary from camp to camp, depending on the nature of the work assignments and the church agency in charge. In May 1941 as C.O.s began to arrive at the first CPS camps, church officials assumed that the men would participate in the program for one year, equal the time required of men in the armed forces. But beginning in August 1941 draft notices were extended to eighteen months and, after the bombing of Pearl Harbor in December 1941, to "the duration and six months."

Since the MCC, BSC, and AFSC had agreed to pay for day-to-day camp operations, each organization collected funds for this purpose from their constituent bodies. The Mennonites used a quota plan, assigning small amounts (ranging from twenty-five to fifty cents per month) to

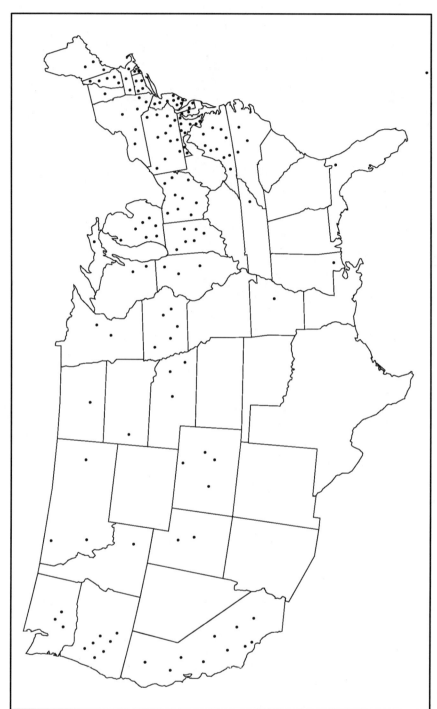

Civilian Public Service locations. (*Adapted from* The CPS Story: An Illustrated History of Civilian Public Service *by Albert N. Keim. Copyright 1990 by Good Books, Intercourse, Pennsylvania. Used by permission. All rights reserved*)

be raised from members of Mennonite churches. Some congregations raised their share of contributions by holding monthly offerings for CPS; others did so by canvassing members. The American Friends Service Committee took the more direct approach of asking families of Friends in CPS to pay approximately thirty-five dollars each month in support of their sons, husbands, and brothers.[28]

During the first two years of Civilian Public Service nearly all of the conscientious objectors in the program were sent to base camps of more than one hundred men where work assignments involved manual labor. Of the first sixty-two camps that opened from May 1941 to November 1942, most were located in the Northeast and Pacific Northwest. Twenty-five camps operated as part of the U.S. Forest Service; another seventeen performed work for the U.S. Soil Conservation Service. Five camps benefited the National Park Service, while a few others aided the Public Health Service, the Bureau of Reclamation, and the General Land Office. Often the men lived in CCC barracks that had only recently been vacated, and most of these sites were isolated from cities and towns. After November 1942 some men were permitted to move from base camps to newly opened detached service units, which Selective Service approved for conscientious objectors eager for more specialized work in mental hospitals and training schools, dairy farming and dairy testing, fire fighting, and scientific research. By January 1944 more men were in detached service than in base camps.[29]

Although the Mennonites, Brethren, and Friends operated most of the CPS camps and units, other agencies also became involved through the National Service Board for Religious Objectors. By 1944 NSBRO had expanded to include directors and council members with thirty-nine organizational affiliations. A number of these groups, including the American Baptist Home Mission Society, the Association of Catholic Conscientious Objectors, the Disciples of Christ, the Evangelical and Reformed churches, and the Methodist Commission on World Peace, opened CPS camps in response to the needs of their own constituencies.[30]

Even before the bombing of Pearl Harbor, Mennonite, Brethren, and Friends' women's organizations across the United States supported conscientious objectors in CPS camps and in prison. Women's sewing societies prepared "camp kits" of bedding, towels, toiletries, stationery, stamps, and other personal items as sending-off gifts for young men assigned to CPS. Groups of churchwomen sent cash, clothing, food, and Christmas gifts to conscientious objectors. Occasionally, women who lived within driving distance of a CPS camp loaded portable sewing machines into cars and spent the day mending assignees' work clothes. In addition to their support of conscientious objectors, some women sent clothing, food, and medical supplies to war victims via nongovernmental relief agencies.[31]

Some women became benefactors to CPS men needing financial help. The Philadelphia headquarters of the Women's International League for Peace and Freedom (WILPF) established a fund to assist jailed C.O.s with bail and made special efforts to communicate to WILPF members what kinds of contributions would be most appreciated by men in CPS. In 1943, after surveying men in Civilian Public Service, WILPF leaders distributed to its membership a wish list. For Friends' camps, the organization solicited basketballs and books on philosophy; for Mennonites, E. Stanley Jones's *Christ and Human Suffering* and the works of Charles Dickens; for Brethren, books on training for reconstruction; and for Catholics, cigarettes, *Catholic World*, and *Thomist Thought*.[32]

Monetary and material aid took many forms. Some women tucked twenty-dollar bills into monthly letters to friends and relatives; others paid assignees' life insurance premiums until they were released from CPS.[33] In 1942 a Methodist woman from the small town of Minneapolis, Kansas, wrote to CPS leaders of her efforts to persuade other women in her congregation to support conscientious objectors:

> Our [Methodist] women's magazine urged us to send money and gifts to our World Peace Commission to be used for the CPS camps. I called their attention to it and they voted to send $5.00 out of the treasury. But some A No. 1 propagandists got wind of it and raised a furor and now the leaders are confused and don't know what to do. Our pastor's wife suggests we drop it to keep down trouble. But I assure you that a few of us will do something; I hope several times over that amount. Also, as I have opportunity, I will see that the truth is given out.[34]

Like many women who supported men in Civilian Public Service, her action represented a defiance of cultural norms. Also a member of the local chapter of the Woman's Christian Temperance Union, she enlisted that group in sending needed items to conscientious objectors in Colorado: men's overalls and coats, and pictures to brighten their camp's office, dining room, and infirmary.[35] Gestures like these helped to stretch camp budgets and were taken as a sign by isolated C.O.s that someone in the outside world cared about them.

As the war stretched on, the costs of the expanding program severely strained the financial resources of its sponsors. Gradually the initial enthusiasm of conscientious objectors for CPS gave way to concerns about whether it provided opportunities for work of national importance as a justifiable alternative to military service. As criticism mounted from both within and outside the program, CPS administrators became sensitive to the ideological gulf separating C.O.s from other Americans. With difficulty, leaders of CPS sought to demonstrate to a skeptical public that almost all American conscientious objectors were patriots as well as sincere Christians. In 1943 the Mennonite Central Committee, which administered CPS camps on behalf of Mennonites, Amish, and related church groups, asserted that "CPS work has meaning to the men who perform it as an expression of loyalty and love to their country, and of their desire to make a contribution to its welfare."[36]

Civilian Public Service administrators, obliged to accommodate more and more newly drafted C.O.s, continued to open additional camps and units. In 1943 the number of new sites opening across the country peaked at fifty-four. No one knew how much longer the war would go on, and in this climate of uncertainty, the Mennonite, Brethren, and Quaker church leaders who operated most of the camps found it more and more difficult to justify the program to conscientious objectors.

Dissension within the camps mounted. Some men, strenuously opposed to conscription, considered prison a better alternative than CPS. Others thought that noncombatant military service might be preferable. Since the majority of jobs in CPS required neither technical nor professional skills, many C.O.s felt they were merely putting in time and questioned whether their assignments really constituted "work of national importance." Others would have gladly chosen noncombatant work in the first place if Selective Service had guaranteed them assignments in the armed forces' medical corps, but decided to enter CPS to avoid being assigned to engineering or quartermaster corps services.[37]

Still others objected to working for the federal government indefinitely without wages. Initially, church leaders who had helped design Civilian Public Service had agreed that men in the camps would work without pay. This concession was largely an effort to dissociate CPS from military control. In the best of all possible worlds, peace church leaders believed, CPS would be "wholly under civilian . . . and church direction, with freedom to direct the life of the camps."[38] Thus the churches had promised Selective Service that they would absorb the entire cost of operating the camps, including maintenance of the men, who would receive from sponsoring church agencies small monthly allowances to cover the cost of incidentals.

This arrangement wore thin. Ultimately, one out of every fourteen men assigned to CPS left the program. Most requested reclassification as noncombatants, claiming that their families could not make ends meet or citing disillusionment with a government bureaucracy that conscripted their labor but offered no compensation.[39]

A Unique Church-State Partnership

Within Civilian Public Service, the religious and ethnic mix of assignees varied by locale. The Mennonite Central Committee operated sixty-five camps and units, more than the Friends, Brethren, or any other group. These Mennonite-sponsored camps, with a total of 5,830 men, included large contingents of Mennonite inductees, most of whom came from rural backgrounds. Though some had completed college and graduate programs, many had had no formal education beyond high school, and the Old Order Amish and Holdeman men rarely had more than an eighth-grade education. By contrast, C.O.s in Brethren and Friends camps tended to be better educated and less communally oriented than those in Mennonite camps.[40]

The war's popularity meant that the three historic peace churches operating CPS had the backing of only part of their constituencies. Studies conducted after the war showed that Brethren and Quakers had remarkably low rates of entry into CPS—about 10 percent of drafted Friends and 8 percent of drafted Brethren took part in the program.[41] Even among the Mennonites, only about 46 percent of drafted men entered the program, while an additional 14 percent, also C.O.s, entered noncombatant military service. As historian Paul Toews observes, during the Second World War Mennonites "clearly were not encased in an ideological straightjacket which automatically passed on the theology and practice of nonresistance."[42] Community standards, parental preferences, and pronouncements from the pulpit varied widely.

Of the approximately 12,000 men who served in CPS, 4,665 identified themselves as Mennonites (including the Amish and Holdeman); 1,353 were from the Church of the Brethren, and 951 belonged to the Society of Friends. After these three groups, the denominations best represented in Civilian Public Service were the Methodists, with nearly 700 men, and Jehovah's Witnesses, Baptists, Presbyterians, Catholics, and Lutherans. In total, the men assigned to CPS reported affiliations with 231 denominations and faiths, ranging from African Methodist Episcopal to Zoroastrianism.[43] This mix, distributed more broadly in the AFSC and BSC camps than in the relatively cohesive Mennonite camps, produced a cacophony of voices about what Civilian Public Service could and should strive to achieve.[44]

Some men who spent years in the program came to loathe it as an affront to civilized society since, in their experience, government officials saw them as troublemakers and aimed to keep them out of public view. In 1979 Gordon Zahn, a Catholic C.O. and sociologist, published a searing account of his CPS experience. Zahn drew parallels to World War II's concentration camps, even while acknowledging that in Civilian Public Service there had been "no brutal guards, no barbed wire, no dogs, no gas chambers." Regardless, he argued, the men in CPS "were considered dangerous to the war-supporting consensus simply because they thought too much."[45]

It was true that the U.S. government did operate a few camps that invited such analogies. From 1943 to 1945 Selective Service opened four CPS camps independent of church administration at Mancos, Colorado; Lapine, Oregon; Germfask, Michigan; and Minersville, California. Although some C.O.s welcomed the emergence of government-administered service, these sites soon earned the reputation of being "dumping grounds" for misfits and for C.O.s charged with insubordination or unsatisfactory work performance. Men at church-operated camps who were uncooperative were sometimes transferred against their will to these government camps.[46]

As an institutional experiment forged in a time of national crisis, Civilian Public Service did not satisfy many of the men it sought to protect. This was inevitable, given the compromises that had been structured into the program before the United States formally entered the war. In 1946 the American Friends Service Committee withdrew from CPS due to disenchantment with the punitive aspects of the program, and the historic peace church officials who continued to administer most of the CPS camps and units were left to grapple with the logistical problems of demobilizing thousands of conscientious objectors.[47]

The program's shortcomings were obvious. A Mennonite C.O. who had invested three years in Civilian Public Service commented that it grew up in an emergency, on short notice, within very realistic limitations. Why CPS leaders have defended the planning and projects of CPS so vigorously, as if they were a precious brainchild, I have never been able to see.

Why not say—this was the best thing that could be worked out on short notice, with a government having no experience with alternate service and afraid to move, and worked out within the framework of adverse public opinion. In trying to improve it we have run up against the wall of government conservatism and lack of interest. Then when we have said this, we should say it again.[48]

These words, uttered in January 1946, anticipated the interpretations of CPS that scholars would offer in subsequent decades. Civilian Public Service was a unique church-state partnership that from the beginning had critics from both within the Roosevelt administration and among antiwar circles. Selective Service, which retained broad powers of authority over the program, persistently viewed the historic peace churches as agents of the government. General Lewis B. Hershey, director of Selective Service, argued that alternative provisions were an indulgence granted by a benevolent state. This outlook clashed, over scores of administrative issues, with the perspective of church leaders who were responsible for day-to-day operations and who insisted that the claim of a conscientious objector against participation in war was not simply a privilege, but a moral right.[49]

Despite these tensions, many C.O.s tried to make the best of the program, believing that it would aid them in making a tangible witness for peace. Although World War II C.O.s faced harassment and verbal abuse, physical violence against them was uncommon. The historic peace church officials had the weight of federal law on their side, and they worked to put a good face on the program, utilizing offers of help from American citizens—oftentimes, women—who embraced the cause of conscientious objection.

2 Am I Worth Dying For?

Few Americans questioned the gender-laden stereotype that war compelled men to go forth and fight to protect their women and children.[1] The 10 May 1942 issue of the *New York Times Magazine* featured an article about Civilian Public Service, which a year earlier had opened its first camp at Patapsco, Maryland. The writer recounted his conversation with a young CPS man named Walt, who spoke of Mennonite farming practices and the woman he wanted to marry. The journalist responded: "Look, Walt, you have this harrow and girl and the farm crop your brothers are bringing in. Whose job is it to protect these things you own and this girl you want?"[2] An Illinois man who detested the presence of a newly established CPS camp near his home made the same point, though more bitterly: "When this bloody conflict is over . . . this gang of traitors can return home hale and hardy to their cars, their girls and wives, to their good American life while the parents of true Americans can look ahead to a life of broken hearts."[3]

Ultimately, Americans would sacrifice for war aims the lives of 405,399 sons and brothers. Even more Americans —670,846—would be wounded. Civilians spent the years of war burdened with worry about their loved ones. The notion of wartime sacrifice became imbued with theological meaning as Americans at home identified emotionally with soldiers abroad. Eleanor Roosevelt reportedly carried in her purse this prayer:

> Dear Lord
> Lest I continue
> My complacent way

Help me to remember
Somewhere out there
A man died for me today.
— As long as there be war
I then must
Ask and answer
Am I worth dying for?[4]

Civilians demonstrated their "moral worthiness" for the cause by relinquishing "selfish" desires and supporting wage and price freezes, rationing, and higher taxes. An enduring image of World War II is that millions of Americans went all out in common spirit and purpose, devoting themselves — no questions asked — to winning the war.[5]

Government and industry officials launched campaigns of unprecedented scope and intensity to galvanize public support of the war effort, calling on "women, married or single, with or without home responsibilities," to take jobs.[6] "Work for women is an old, not a new thing," implored one author who argued that American women should consider adding war work to their domestic obligations.[7] After Pearl Harbor, women found themselves subject to new and often contradictory pressures. Government agencies responsible for mobilizing support for the war exhorted mothers to ensure family stability, urged workers to devote themselves to war production, and counseled volunteers in how to raise the morale of American troops. These powerful appeals for women to do short-term war work reinforced the idea that they were the standard bearers of a moral America.[8]

Prescriptive literature for women of all ages and circumstances called for a reordering of priorities. A book published in 1942 for American mothers advised: "You are one of many pulling together. . . . You are participating in the most important of all causes right now. You are helping to win the war."[9] To demonstrate their patriotism, American women sewed bandages, planted victory gardens, canned food, took courses in first aid, participated in blood drives, and collected money for defense bonds.

Yet the women who took part in Civilian Public Service gave alternative responses to questions of citizenship. Their reply to the question "Am I worth dying for?" was "No!" In making choices that gave substance to that conviction, they were acting in a venerable tradition of American peace activism.[10]

Sticks and Stones: Growing up Pacifist in America

The women who associated themselves with Civilian Public Service acted as nonconformists in relation to the larger home front culture. Yet paradoxically, they conformed quite readily to the values and expectations of religious pacifist communities. Stability characterized their family structures, and parents were unusually successful in transmitting values to the next generation. Within these cultures of nonconformity, many young women formed deeply held convictions that would enable them to make choices against the grain of the broader culture.[11]

Pacifist women on the American home front spurned what historian Paul Fussell has termed the "high-mindedness" of America's popular support for the war.[12] They did not participate in voluntarism such as entertaining troops with USO camp shows or promoting war bond drives. They thought of such activities as coerced support of military authority and advocated, instead, a nonconformist ethic of peacemaking. For most of them, such attitudes toward war and civic responsibility had long been in the making.

As children, many had absorbed religious values that would remain constant throughout their lives. The Mennonites and Brethren, and to a lesser extent the Friends, prized nonconformity to the larger society. In many of these homes antiwar thought was derived from biblical teachings and from internationalist perspectives. One woman, asked to reflect on major influences in her life, cited lessons learned from her parents and grandparents: "We grew up with stories of ancestors who did not participate in the Civil War or in World War I." Another recalled: "My parents were opposed to war. I remember my father ordering a booklet in the early '40s, titled *Dare We Break the Vicious Cycle of Fighting Evil With Evil?* [written by the American clergyman Harry Emerson Fosdick], and handing out copies to people who came to his grocery store." And another remembered: "My values were formed by my parents, both by example and teaching. I distinctly remember their distress regarding Japanese internment during the war. I remember Dad wanting to relate to [German] POWs if possible."[13]

As they reached adolescence, many of these youngsters found the world of public high school to be isolating and even downright unfriendly. During the late 1930s and early 1940s, as Americans kept watch on developments in Asia and Europe, educators and military strategists collaborated on programs for preteens and teenagers that emphasized duty to country. The federal Office of Education published the biweekly

Education for Victory, which was read by school administrators eager to integrate students' education with the war effort. Another influential publication, *The American Teacher*, the journal of the American Federation of Teachers, advocated that war themes be taught across the curriculum, from history to health, science to spelling. Seventy percent of the nation's high schools joined the Victory Corps program, which was established in 1942 by the federal government and funded by local school systems and community boosters. The Victory Corps recruited both boys and girls for scrap collection drives, war stamp and bond sales, and conservation programs. And across America, girls flocked to extracurricular character-building programs such as the Girl Scouts, Camp Fire Girls, and Girl Reserves (a junior division of the YWCA), all of which linked religious principles with civic duty.[14]

Pressure to conform was intense; many students literally wore their patriotism on their sleeve, sporting arm bands that indicated membership in the Victory Corps or in local spin-off programs, sometimes called Victory Councils or Victory Cadets. School-sponsored campaigns in support of the war marked pacifist students as different from their peers and became occasions for ad hoc conscientious objection. One woman, a Mennonite, recalled her discomfort when, as a high school student, she learned that school officials were planning to dismiss school for a scrap metal drive. She asked to be excused from the activity, and her principal, a fellow Mennonite, agreed.[15]

Pacifist students *and* teachers often faced negative repercussions if they refused to participate in war boosterism on school time. Some women dropped career plans to teach when they realized the pressure they would be under to support war bond sales. Esther Lehrman, who taught school near an air base in Idaho, recalled that she did not discuss her views about the war at work because the husbands and fiancés of her colleagues were servicemen. Lehrman participated in school-sponsored scrap metal drives, although her conscience bothered her. Later she reflected, "I thought my job depended upon doing the things that were expected, and I was afraid to stand up for what I believed was right."[16] Still, she tried to blunt the impact of school-sponsored militarism:

> In school we were to push the buying of war stamps and bonds, and every Friday there was sort of a contest to see how much each class could buy. Children brought money to school to buy war stamps. Different classes had posters, etc., to encourage children to buy them and

to compete with other classes. I felt a little guilty about this and didn't know how to get out of doing it. Instead of making a poster with war-like things, I made one with parachutes. If children brought stamp money, they could put up a parachute on the poster. I guess I felt that parachutes were saving lives instead of taking life, [so I avoided] putting war tanks or guns on the poster.[17]

After three years, the strain of wartime teaching in a small town caused Lehrman to quit her job and to join conscientious objectors who were working in a mental hospital in Ypsilanti, Michigan. After the war, she finished college and became part of a Mennonite-sponsored voluntary service unit in Puerto Rico. She never returned to teaching.[18]

Pacifist students learned early that taking a minority stance could have painful consequences. At Chester High School in North Manchester, Indiana, the principal, a World War I veteran, made students march to their classes and face east to salute the flag every morning. One of his students, the daughter of a Church of the Brethren minister, refused to come forward each week in study hall to buy war stamps. She remembered: "He made fun of me in front of the whole school."[19] At Windom High School in Kansas, a Mennonite girl and her younger brother were called "Hitler's children" by their classmates for refusing to buy war stamps. "You didn't want anyone to know that you knew German or were of German ancestry," she recalled.[20]

Being of German descent and espousing pacifist views did make some students doubly vulnerable to persecution. The city of Newton, Kansas, and the surrounding rural area had a sizable Mennonite population, and most local Mennonite children came from homes where parents spoke German as well as English. During the First World War vigilantes had streaked Mennonite-owned homes, barns, and stores with yellow paint, and vandals in Newton and nearby communities painted Mennonite storefronts yellow again in 1941 and 1942.[21] For some students, the pressure was excruciating. At Newton High School, a Mennonite ninth grader was humiliated by her homeroom teacher because she was the only one in class who did not bring scrap metal to the all-school drive.[22] Betty Regier Wasser, who also attended Newton High, reported that "we conscientious objectors were given such a hard time that my dad, a college professor, had me skip my senior year and start college a year early."[23] Two of her Mennonite classmates did the same.

Some pacifist students were recalcitrant. Karolyn Kaufman, a seventh grader in Newton at the time of Pearl Harbor, refused to buy defense stamps, remained seated during the singing of patriotic songs at assemblies, and hid in a culvert on the way home from school to avoid incensed classmates. But two years of this tension was enough. In September 1943 she was part of an exodus of Mennonite students out of the Newton school system to the Mennonite Bible Academy, a private high school located on the Bethel College campus north of town. Teenagers looking to break out of the stigma of their school identities welcomed the reopening of the academy, which had been closed since 1927. In the fall of 1943 forty-six students enrolled; a year later, the school's census jumped to seventy. By the end of the war Mennonite educators in Lancaster and Johnstown, Pennsylvania; Culp, Arkansas; Kalona, Iowa; and Salem, Oregon, had established private high schools for Mennonite students in those communities as well.[24]

Throughout these years leaders of the historic peace churches debated how they might help public school students who felt pressured to take part in war-related activities. They had begun the process of building alternative institutions well before the United States entered World War II, and in 1943 Betty Jacob, a Pennsylvania Quaker activist, worked with Friends, Brethren, and Mennonite organizations to develop a High School Civilian Service program. While the folk wisdom of many school administrators was that the sale of war stamps and bond drives inspired patriotism and thrift among students, a few rejected the national high school Victory Corps as too militaristic.[25] Promoters of the High School Civilian Service program advocated it as an alternative that would encourage public service minus the jingoistic rhetoric. They hoped to create spaces in which students could, in good conscience, express their altruism and civic responsibility. This impulse mirrored the better-known Civilian Public Service program for draft-age men, in which American conscientious objectors were building roads, fighting forest fires, serving as guinea pigs in medical experiments, and attending to the mentally ill.

Public Perceptions of American C.O.s

Throughout the war American magazines and newspapers published thousands of articles on Civilian Public Service. Many of these were feature stories filed by reporters who were curious about the program and who covered happenings at local CPS sites. Administrators of the camps and units welcomed journalists and treated them hospitably, interpreting the whys and wherefores of conscientious objection and try-

Lew Ayres, star of the film *All Quiet on the Western Front*, en route to a CPS camp in Oregon, told reporters in Sacramento, California, that because of his idealistic principles he would not wear an army uniform. (*Associated Press/Wide World Photos*)

ing to avert negative press coverage. Civilian Public Service camp directors and staff developed considerable skill in dealing with journalists. On 15 May 1941, the day the first camp was scheduled to open near Patapsco, Maryland, fifty-four photographers and reporters descended on the place, two to each C.O. assigned there.[26]

The mainstream press also gave substantial coverage to the case of Hollywood star Lew Ayres, who became a conscientious objector as a result of his work in the film *All Quiet on the Western Front*. In the spring of 1942 Ayres entered Civilian Public Service, but after several months of forestry work in Oregon, World War II's best-known conscientious objector left for noncombatant service in the army medical corps.[27]

Advocates of C.O.s with a flair for public relations sometimes whipped up interest in their cause. The poet laureate William Stafford, a Church of the Brethren member whose four years in CPS included stints in California and three other states, liked to tell the story of a "forthright young pacifist" who planned to marry her fiancé in the rustic setting of a

Forest Service camp. As the day approached, Stafford said, she "wrote an announcement of the wedding, prominently mentioning Civilian Public Service, and delivered it, in person, and with a lecture on the worth of C.O.s, to the society editor of the *Santa Barbara News-Press.*"[28]

Antiwar perspectives also filtered into public consciousness through popular novels that featured conscientious objectors as lead characters. Ann Chidester's *No Longer Fugitive*, published in 1943, depicted an insecure young man who left his small Minnesota community to avoid facing his draft board, which he was sure would treat him unsympathetically because two of his brothers were serving in the military. Granville Hicks's book *Behold Trouble* portrayed a depraved, nonreligious C.O. who caused an uproar in his community. But Hicks made clear that his fictional character was atypical and did not epitomize the values of men in Civilian Public Service camps.

Throughout World War II conscientious objectors in CPS camps were easy targets for verbal hostility. Healthy young men in civilian clothing were conspicuous as they traveled in towns on camp business, transferred from one CPS location to another, or took time off during government-approved furloughs. One alumnus of Civilian Public Service recalled the "relative ignominy and disgrace" of the program and claimed that he and fellow conscientious objectors were "fourth-class citizens."[29] On occasions when they were visible to the public, C.O.s were vulnerable to stereotypes that challenged their masculinity. Gordon Zahn, writing three decades later of his World War II experiences, remembered that civilian project managers at his base camp complained that the government was asking them to supervise "a bunch of yellow bastards."[30] William Stafford reported hearing a Forest Service employee say to a buddy in a California ranger station: "I wish I was superintendent of that camp; I'd line 'em up and uh-uh-uh . . . (making sounds of a machine gun)."[31]

Dorothy Detzer, a peace activist who throughout World War II lobbied congressional officials on behalf of the Women's International League for Peace and Freedom, recounted in her autobiography some of the low moments of being a war objector. As if in refrain, Americans incredulous of her stance would ask: "Now tell me, what would you peace people have done, had you been running the government at the time of Pearl Harbor? Just how would you have stopped the Japs then?" Detzer, for whom pacifism was a consistent and morally defensible stance, considered such questions to be rhetorical vehicles for ridicule.[32] Other C.O.s, for sport, kept logs of the outrageous names tossed their way: "slacker," "Fascist,"

"Nazi," "Communist," "spy," "fifth columnist." "Conchie" came into wide usage as shorthand for "conscientious objector," but C.O. insiders used the term as readily as their critics. At Hagerstown, Maryland, CPS men assigned to soil conservation named their camp dog "Conchie."[33]

C.O.s in Civilian Public Service camps were susceptible to insinuations that they were shirking their duties as men. Some coped with these pressures better than others. For many, the communal nature of camp life served as a buffer against local antagonism. Harry van Dyck, a C.O. from Nebraska, recalled the close relationships and tight cliques of CPS. "A spirit of male camaraderie dominated our psyches," he remembered, much like the bonding that occurred in military settings.[34] Gordon Zahn reported that assignees at the Catholic-operated camp at Warner, New Hampshire, binged on alcohol as a way of proving that they were "as manly and as Catholic as anyone else."[35] Alcohol usage was hardly limited to the camp at Warner; in 1943 a Quaker observer noted that "drinking has been a problem in most of the Friends' camps for quite a while . . . though a good deal of drinking means maybe ten percent who occasionally drink, and maybe two or three individuals who occasionally get drunk."[36]

Incidents of homosexuality, too, occurred in CPS settings, vexing officials who were responsible for maintaining camp standards. But celibacy was the norm. Reports of conscientious objectors who visited prostitutes were rare. In van Dyck's experience, contacts between assignees and women were limited, and most of the men he knew in camp were "unattached but yearning."[37]

Throughout the war peace church leaders placed tight restrictions on the men in CPS, following orders from Selective Service officials, who warned that "the assignee . . . has no free time. . . . Hours of work, of rising and retiring, meals, meetings, etc., as well as liberty, leave, and furlough, are all subject to control."[38] As early as 1941 some CPS administrators tried to rid camps of privately owned cars, "lest people get the false impression that our boys can run around at will."[39] Before December 1942, however, when nationwide gas rationing took effect, such appeals had little impact. At some of the smaller CPS camps, located off the beaten track of Selective Service overseers, camp directors imposed few regulations. A dietitian arriving in May 1942 at the AFSC camp in Royalston, Massachusetts, found that assignees there enjoyed unchecked liberties: "The camp car goes into town to the movies four or five times a week, and twice on Sunday for church and movies. No charge is made,

Conscientious objector in staff quarters at Cleveland State Hospital, Ohio, with letter and photo of fiancée. (*Mennonite Central Committee Photograph Collection, IX-13-2, Archives of the Mennonite Church, Goshen, Indiana*)

either. . . . Girlfriends come and go freely—one just stayed a whole week. . . . Over a third of the boys have cars. There is no limit on weekend leave—one boy has been gone every weekend except in fire season."[40]

Faced with continual public relations concerns, however, CPS officials tightened camp discipline and advised assignees to maintain low profiles. Occasionally, however, dramatic events enabled men in CPS to demonstrate their sincerity to skeptical neighbors. In March 1942 a tornado devastated Lacon, Illinois, killing fourteen persons and injuring a hundred more. C.O.s assigned to the camp at nearby Henry, Illinois, worked for several months to reconstruct the town.

Some communities took little notice of the C.O. presence at nearby camps; others reacted with great displeasure. At Coshocton, Ohio, an AFSC-administered camp had more than its share of problems because the camp was located in an area where many Amish and Mennonite residents claimed conscientious objector status. As a result, the local draft board had to rely heavily on the rest of the population to meet its quota for military inductees. Community resentment was palpable. Every morning, schoolchildren passing by CPS men doing soil conservation work hurled insults at them, incited by their bus driver and, presumably, their parents.[41] At Merom, Indiana, a CPS camp opened in June 1941 to protests from townspeople that the conscientious objectors would be taking work away from employees of the Works Progress Administration. Angry members of the American Legion threatened to run the new arrivals out of town. The furor eventually died down, but in a few cases of extreme community antagonism, CPS administrators closed down or relocated camps.[42]

Sometimes race relations were a significant factor in the tensions that arose between CPS camps and nearby communities. In December 1942 conscientious objectors at the CPS camp in Placerville, California, tried to ship a large package of handcrafted Christmas toys to children living in a Japanese internment camp in Arizona. Pandemonium resulted as rumors spread throughout the community that the men were sending dynamite, guns, or other subversive materials to the Japanese. The men of the Placerville camp managed to send the gift, but only after a lengthy exchange with community officials, in which the sheriff told the camp's assistant director: "It may have been all right to make toys, but I can't see why you fellows should want to send them to those dirty, yellow-bellied sons-of-bitches when there are lots of needy *white* children around here."[43]

Many Christian pacifists tried to make contact with Japanese internees, sending Christmas bundles and writing supportive letters, for example, or trying to secure the release of Japanese American students so they could attend college.[44] One Japanese American from California, George Yamada, felt that support more directly than most, for he himself was a conscientious objector who had been assigned to Civilian Public Service just days before Pearl Harbor. Kermit Sheets, a CPS assignee who served with Yamada in forestry work at Cascade Locks, Oregon, recalled the CPS men's reaction when Yamada received the order to go to a relocation site:

> Wow, that camp blew apart! Because here was a guy already as isolated as you could be. We knew George, he was a conscientious objector, for crying out loud! He wasn't going to send messages to Japan which would make them shoot us! The whole thing was absolutely ridiculous.

> Then we had loads of meetings as to how we were going to handle it when they came for George. It got extremely tense, verging on melodramatic, for the feelings that were there. People wondering how many people should lie down in front of the car that was to take him away.

> In the end, George was ordered to transfer from the Locks to the CPS camp at Colorado Springs. I guess it was recognized that he was interred as much in a CPS camp as he would have been in a relocation center. But the move was ordered because of George's race and of course he recognized that. However, he didn't want to cause disruption that would end up with other guys being picked up for something they would do to resist his being picked up. So he went.[45]

On the other side of the country, southern prejudices reared in September 1942 when the American Friends Service Committee decided to move its CPS camp at Patapsco, Maryland, to the coastal community of Powellsville, Maryland. Powellsville leaders warned CPS officials not to bring along the camp's lone black conscientious objector. But the rest of the men in the camp told CPS officials that if he could not go to Powellsville, neither would they. At the request of the black C.O., the AFSC transferred him to a detached service unit at Cheltenham, Maryland, before the Patapsco camp moved to Powellsville.[46]

Three years later, AFSC officials faced more serious consequences over racial tensions in Orlando, Florida, where CPS men involved in hook-

TABLE 2.1. Questionnaire and Oral History Respondents' Primary Association with CPS

Wartime Experience[a]	Number of Women	Percent of Sample
Wife, fiancée, girlfriend[b]	108	60
CPS camp dietician	15	8
CPS camp nurse	13	7
Staff member for AFSC, BSC, MCC, or NSBRO[c]	19	11
Member of women's CPS unit or coed relief training unit	19	11
Other[d]	6	3
Total	180	100

[a]For many women, these categories overlapped during the war. For example, some dietitians, nurses, staff members, and women's unit members became engaged to and married CPS men during and after the war. See Table 3.1 on marital status.

[b]34 percent of the women in this category found employment at mental hospitals where conscientious objectors were assigned to work.

[c]Includes both paid and unpaid workers.

[d]Includes peace activists and benefactors of men in CPS.

worm eradication tested Jim Crow laws by sponsoring a graduation party for local black high school students. Community leaders were outraged to learn of dancing at the party between white men and black female students, and the camp's assistant director was forced to transfer to another CPS unit. As a result of continued local hostility, the Orlando unit relocated to Gainesville.[47]

Such incidents, though troubling, did not pose an insurmountable challenge to this program of alternative service. During World War II Americans were inclined to give conscientious objectors in CPS the benefit of the doubt, even though they approved the national call to arms for themselves and their family members.[48] In contrast to the negative stereotypes of C.O.s that had been prevalent during the 1930s, most Americans in the 1940s tolerated C.O.s who performed government-sanctioned work. During 1943 and 1944 psychologist Leo Crespi of Princeton University conducted a series of studies to measure the attitudes of Americans toward conscientious objectors. More than three-quarters of those surveyed nationwide favored wages and family allotments for C.O.s en-

TABLE 2.2. Questionnaire and Oral History Respondents' Wartime Religious Affiliation

Denomination	Number of Women	Percent of Sample
Mennonite	110	61
Church of the Brethren	17	9
Society of Friends	9	5
Methodist	8	4
Presbyterian	4	2
Amish	3	2
Baptist	3	2
Church of God in Christ, Mennonite	3	2
Evangelical and Reformed	3	2
Roman Catholic	3	2
Congregational	2	1
Episcopal	2	1
Advent Christian	1	.5
Church of Christ	1	.5
Disciples of Christ	1	.5
Evangelical United Brethren	1	.5
German Baptist Brethren	1	.5
Union Church	1	.5
No affiliation	7	4
Total	180	100

gaged in Civilian Public Service. Yet, ironically, most who expressed these opinions believed that they were in the minority.[49]

Wartime Choices

The women who became part of Civilian Public Service encountered reactions ranging from animosity and scorn to admiration. Women chose CPS for a variety of reasons. Some craved travel and adventure; others simply wanted to be with husbands or friends. These motives paralleled those of American women in their early and middle twenties who volunteered for military duty. A survey conducted in the mid-1980s of more than seven hundred female veterans of World War II — nurses, WACs (army), WAVES (navy), SPARS (Coast Guard), and marines — found

TABLE 2.3. Questionnaire and Oral History Respondents' Wartime Educational Status

Wartime Educational Status[a]	Number of Women	Percent of Sample
Grade school	6	3
High school	45	25
Postsecondary work[b]	77	43
College/university graduate	46	26
Postgraduate work	6	3
Total	180	100

[a]Denotes highest educational level attained by the end of World War II.

[b]Includes college- or university-level course work, business school training, and nurses' training.

that enlisted women identified patriotism and wanting to put their skills to good use as prime motivating factors. The veterans also recalled their desire to "try something different" and to travel. A few admitted that they had wanted to escape unpleasant circumstances in family or work settings.[50] To a large extent, pacifist women on the home front shared these impulses. In addition, many of them identified strongly with Christian traditions that provided both the language and justification for taking an antiwar stance. In Civilian Public Service they would find an outlet for their interests and abilities.

Through 1946 the supporters of World War II conscientious objectors — part of a large wave of American wartime migration — would follow loved ones to CPS settings across the country via train, bus, automobile, motorcycle, or by hitchhiking. As women on the home front, they were on the receiving end of propagandistic appeals to "be the sort of women that men would be proud to protect."[51] Yet these women belonged to a cultural minority, and they would defy expectations, for they were citizens whose views on war were considered anomalous by almost everyone else.

3

No Girl Should Marry
into This Kind of Life

Louise Wilson of Amherst, Massachusetts, was one of the first women to follow her husband into Civilian Public Service. In July 1941 the thirty-five-year-old Quaker woman arrived at Patapsco, Maryland, with her infant daughter, Lucy, and dog, Glory, to assist her husband, Eugene "Bill" Wilson, in directing the newly opened AFSC camp. Bill Wilson, who was above draft age, was a short-term volunteer for the American Friends Service Committee, and he and Louise had decided to send their two older children to a summer camp in the Pocono mountains while they worked at Patapsco. Defending these arrangements to her skeptical parents, Louise Wilson explained that "I could not just do this any other summer. . . . These [CPS] camps will be made or lost before next May."[1]

Conscientious objectors at Patapsco lived in the public eye, for the camp was located in a state park, adjacent to both U.S. Highway 1 and a main line of the B&O railroad. Media and Selective Service scrutiny of the newly opened camp were intense. No one was more curious about the C.O.s at Patapsco than the soldiers stationed at nearby Camp Meade. Two weeks after her arrival, Louise Wilson wrote home:

> The army has been going by all day, again. I was cleaning baby's shoes at the bathroom window and heard [a soldier] say 'Geez, they got dames!' Glory barked steadily at them, really seeming ferocious, and I went to the door and called her. Just as I did, they had the order to rest, so they all stood and stared. I got her in and smiled and said, 'Sorry my dog is such a poor pacifist, boys.' But the boys didn't change expression.[2]

Louise and Bill Wilson found it easier to laugh off popular misconceptions about Civilian Public Service than the negative reactions they received from their own family members. Both had brothers in military service, and during the summer of 1941, the Wilsons conceded that they did not expect their families to agree with their convictions; nevertheless, they wrote long letters home explaining why they were aligning themselves with conscientious objectors.[3] Bill's mother reacted angrily, calling her son a fanatic. As the summer came to a close, Louise confided to a friend that her husband's mother was "so ashamed of us that she can hardly stand it. . . . [But] I have smoldered in private and taken all she has had to say for eleven years and I suppose this can go by, also."[4]

Louise Wilson recounted her experiences as a CPS camp follower by writing vivid letters throughout the summer, which she intended to be a record of the camp in its historic first year. In some respects her encounter with Civilian Public Service is typical of the fifteen hundred or more women who from 1941 to 1947 joined husbands or fiancés at Civilian Public Service settings across the country.[5] Like Louise Wilson, many of them shared the ideological commitments of their partners, and their decisions represented political activism. Many had young children, and they struggled to combine the demands of caring for infants or toddlers with other responsibilities. From Patapsco, Wilson wrote home of her fears of "not earning my way, . . . for I give so much time to [the baby] that I do not give much to the camp."[6] Other pacifist mothers echoed this sentiment. And, like Wilson, many experienced the burden of strained or broken relations with disapproving family members.

Yet on balance, the early CPS experiences of Louise Wilson were unique. She enjoyed privileges — most notably, financial security — that the vast majority of CPS wives did not. She could take comfort in the fact that her husband was beyond draft age, and she knew that the routines of family life would be disrupted for only a few months. Wilson's exuberant and idealistic feelings about Civilian Public Service on the eve of America's entry into war differed from the stoicism that would be expressed later by women whose financial resources had become depleted while their C.O. husbands were conscripted to camps for "the duration and six months."

Camp Followers in Historical Perspective

Feminist scholar Cynthia Enloe, in a wide-ranging critique of military organizations, has traced the historic image of the camp follower to seventeenth-century England, when "women traveling with an army . . . ran the risk of being disciplined or disparaged as a common whore." Enloe argues that while such women have long contributed essential services as wives, cooks, laundresses, and nurses during the waging of campaigns, historically they have been barely tolerated by military commanders and been considered outcasts by society.[7]

Scholars interested in the political outlook of women in wartime have examined how family relationships shape attitude and behavior. Historian Mary Beth Norton has studied eighteenth-century patriot and loyalist women to determine how their actions led to a "partial breakdown and reinterpretation of gender roles" during the American Revolution. Assessing the experiences of camp followers on both sides of the war, Norton suggests that wives who joined their spouses at military encampments lacked alternative means of financial support and thus acted out of necessity rather than political activism.[8] Drew Gilpin Faust, in a study of Confederate women, has argued that the Civil War's devastating effects on soldiers' families contributed to a demoralized South; in Faust's view, ideologies of paternalism and sacrifice became unbearable burdens for many Southern white women faced with "the possibility of starvation for themselves and their families and the likelihood of death or injury for a husband or child."[9] Deborah Gorham, examining gender relations and war in the twentieth century, has studied women who abandoned antiwar positions after their sons were drafted in World War I. Like Enloe, Norton, and Faust, Gorham challenges the cultural stereotypes of male-warrior and female-peacemaker and suggests that the historical realities of women caught in war — often in multiple roles as wives, mothers, sisters, and daughters — are far more complex.[10]

During World War II millions of American women in their late teens, twenties, and thirties left home for distant destinations. Military wives trailed their men to stateside army and naval bases, setting up temporary housing in a succession of communities despite the exigencies of rationed gas, worn tires, jammed trains, and scarce housing. Agnes E. Meyer, a columnist for the *Washington Post* who spent 1943 traveling through twenty-seven of the nation's industrial centers, wrote movingly of the impact of war mobilization on family and community relationships: "From one end of the country to the other," she concluded, "it is the children who are paying the price for uncontrolled mass migrations, easy money, unaccustomed hours of work, and the fact that 'Ma' is a welder on the graveyard shift."[11]

TABLE 3.1. Questionnaire and Oral History Respondents' Wartime Marital Status

Marital Status	Number of Women	Percent of Sample
Married (prior to war)	41	23
Married (during war)	86	48
Single (throughout war)	53	29
Total	180	100

Military wives who followed their husbands to stateside camps made living arrangements as best they could. Although the federal Office of War Information discouraged the wives of servicemen from taking up residence near bases, local USO clubs and Traveler's Aid bureaus provided leads on jobs, housing, and volunteer work. Barbara Klaw, an army wife, found job hunting discouraging; an editor at the *Joplin (Mo.) Globe* told her: "No, you girls aren't very good risks from the hiring end."[12]

Still, many camp followers found employment, even if openings were primarily in domestic work. In Colorado Springs and a few other communities where military bases and CPS camps were closely situated, military and C.O. wives lived as neighbors in flats and apartment buildings. Near the CPS camp at Belton, Montana, Selma Unruh, a Mennonite camp follower, worked as a live-in sitter for the three children of a local woman whose husband had gone off to war. The arrangement was unusual, but it was mutually beneficial. Unruh earned room and board while also caring for her own child, the Belton army wife had peace of mind while working outside the home to support her family, and both women enjoyed each other's company.[13]

Wartime Marriage and the Problem of Dependents

The war's disruptive impact on the lives of American military families was mirrored in the dislocation of C.O.s' families. Across the country, couples facing an uncertain future moved up wedding dates to accommodate draft orders. Others postponed marriage plans. In Kansas, Helen Krehbiel, a college student whose fiancé was drafted in 1941, recalled that "priorities shifted. The idea of 'building a little grey home in the West and let the rest of the world go by' seemed very disturbing. There were more important things to be doing."[14] Krehbiel took a teaching job while her fiancé spent two and a half years in Civilian Public

The 1945 wedding of Patricia Kennedy and Harry Burks in Missoula, Montana, was a formal affair with an American G.I. as best man and the wife of a conscientious objector as matron of honor. (*Geraldine Braden, St. Paul, Minnesota*)

Service. After he received a medical discharge, they married, and when the war ended they accepted a two-year relief assignment in Europe with Mennonite Central Committee.

As alternative service stretched from months to years, some couples married during furloughs, and others took their vows at Civilian Public Service camps in the presence of pacifist friends. Like other American war brides, C.O. wives who were separated from their husbands used correspondence to nourish long-distance relationships. One wife worked for a time as a matron in her husband's CPS camp but then moved home and returned to teaching. In a letter she explained: "This way I will not be on charity. . . . We will be better persons for this experience of being separated and making our own way financially. I think we will appreciate each other even more when we live together again."[15] Others found that a husband's draft orders, though unwelcome, provided a nudge to try

The honeymoon of Pearl and Victor Mierau following their 1943 wedding at the CPS camp near Hill City, South Dakota, was a trip around the camp. (*Stan Voth, North Newton, Kansas*)

new things. When DeElda Hershberger's husband left for CPS in 1944, the Iowa woman decided to follow him, first to Colorado and later to Nebraska. She supported herself and her four-year-old son by working as a grocery checker and by accepting monetary gifts from friends and family. In retrospect, Hershberger said, alternative service broadened her outlook: "Our world had been very small until we moved out and saw a larger world needing love and care."[16]

Husbands and fathers assigned to CPS chafed over the lack of government support for their dependents. Most CPS assignees considered the problem of dependents' financial hardship a pressing one, particularly after 1942, when Congress passed the Servicemen's Dependents Allowance Act. This legislation, generous by most accounts, guaranteed benefits to military personnel — including family allowances of approximately fifty dollars per month and obstetric care for military wives. But the new law denied benefits to the families of men assigned to Civilian Public Service.[17]

Leaders of the historic peace churches responsible for administering and financing the program at first gave little thought to the issue of conscientious objectors' dependents since nearly all the earliest assignees were single and childless. In May 1942 Mennonite Central Committee officials recommended that the wives of C.O.s work to support themselves. In fact, most wives did enter the labor force and managed to keep afloat financially. But gradually, CPS officials realized that some wives, children, aged parents, and other dependents would need special assistance. By the fall of 1942 administrators at most camps loosened restrictions on CPS men, permitting them to look for after-hours work that would bring in income for their families.[18]

For many American families, the nation's entry into the war intensified uncertainty about the future. Some C.O. couples tried to conceive children in order to avoid conscription since Selective Service initially exempted fathers. Apparently this was a nationally popular, though doomed, strategy. From 1940 to 1943 the country experienced a baby boomlet as the population of children under the age of five increased 25 percent. But in 1942 Selective Service began to induct childless married men, and later, fathers.[19]

By the end of 1942 the problem of dependency support for C.O.s became acute. While the dependents of a camp assignee could usually live off savings or turn to relatives and friends for assistance for a year or so, the family's financial status was likely to became more precarious with the passage of time. By September 1943, 36 percent of all the men in Civilian Public Service had dependents, and by the end of the war the proportion had risen to 43 percent.[20] Most of these "dependents" were wives who were able to support themselves, but a comprehensive survey conducted in late 1945 by the American Friends Service Committee revealed that men who had not yet been released from CPS were fathers to more than twelve hundred children.[21]

Civilian Public Service assignees agonized over the impoverishment of their families. In April 1945 thirty-two men at a camp in Wellston, Michigan, staged a week-long hunger strike to publicize the problem. They argued unsuccessfully that the cost of their food, estimated at fifty-four cents a day, ought to be disbursed to their dependents.[22] At other camps across the country, some assignees, prompted by their wives, sought reclassification from Civilian Public Service to noncombatant or even combatant status. Their motives varied, but financial incentive was often a factor since opting out of CPS in favor of military service made C.O.s eligible for government benefits.

Most assignees who were Mennonite, Amish, Brethren, or Quaker could turn to their relatives and churches. In addition, a few small religious groups with men in CPS, including the Christadelphians and Disciples of Christ, made serious efforts to assist C.O.s and their dependents. But by far the greatest financial burden fell on persons who espoused C.O. principles independently of church teachings and who had little access to supportive networks. Couples and families who lacked connections to the historic peace churches were often reluctant to ask for help from the agencies responsible for administering CPS.[23]

Some marriages floundered. One assignee wrote to CPS officials that his wife and baby had had to move to his wife's parental home. "I have seen lots of trouble and heard lots about me not caring for my family. . . . [On the subject of CPS] my wife's mind has been changed in the last few months until it makes it very hard on me and her also. . . . My mother-in-law is the one that has said the most to cause trouble between us." In another case, a wife divorced her C.O. husband on the grounds of nonsupport.[24]

The inequities of the Servicemen's Dependents Allowance Act were obvious to those familiar with the problems of C.O. dependents. Administrators at the Philadelphia office of the American Friends Service Committee asked plaintively: "Since conscience is not a crime, why penalize the families of conscientious objectors?"[25] The AFSC leaders hoped that the wages earned by CPS men assigned to farm work could be used to aid needy dependents. Beginning in 1942 private employers of CPS men in agricultural assignments had paid wages into a special fund in the U.S. Treasury; by the time the CPS program ended five years later, the unassigned fund had accumulated to $1,389,144.[26] In 1945 Representative John Sparkman, chair of the House Military Affairs Committee, introduced legislation to authorize Selective Service to pay allowances from the treasury fund to conscientious objectors' families. Two similar measures, introduced in 1943 and 1945, sought to designate the fund for overseas reconstruction work, a plan favored by both the NSBRO and a majority of the men assigned to CPS. But political objections surfaced. Congressman Arthur Winstead of Mississippi suggested that the Civilian Public Service program was "harboring men who merely wanted to get out of military service." Although NSBRO officials maintained that the federal government was morally obligated to support CPS dependents out of the general treasury and that the unspent CPS fund ought to be used for overseas war relief, all three of the bills introduced to disburse the CPS "frozen fund" languished in Congress.[27]

Meanwhile, CPS leaders realized that the peace church agencies would have to address the dependency problem systematically. "It is not sufficient that we say to fathers of families that we will take care of them and that their dependents will not need to suffer hardship," commented Albert Gaeddert, an official of the Mennonite Central Committee. "They cannot plan with such a promise."[28] Beginning in 1944 each of the three major church agencies responsible for CPS raised funds to help support the dependents of men in their respective camps. Any assignee who demonstrated financial need could arrange for his wife to receive from one of the church agencies twenty-five dollars a month, and his children, ten dollars each per month.[29]

While historic peace church leaders appealed to their constituencies for funds to help troubled families, the NSBRO established a council to assist the dependents of men not covered by the churches. The National Service Board for Religious Objectors and the church agencies offered employment counseling, advice regarding day care, and medical assistance. Some branches of the Women's International League for Peace and Freedom joined NSBRO in helping wives of C.O.s to become financially independent.[30]

In all, only 5 percent of CPS assignees ever applied for assistance; to these six hundred men and their families, the peace church agencies and NSBRO paid out about a quarter of a million dollars. As the war came to an end, some antiwar activists, critical of congressional indifference toward the dependents of C.O.s, pointed out that if the families of CPS men had been eligible for the allowances paid to servicemen's dependents, they would have received as much as two million dollars annually in federal aid.[31] By 1947, when Civilian Public Service was phased out, the churches and families of conscientious objectors had contributed $7,202,000 for their support. For the U.S. government, which tallied more than eight million man-days of work and spent just $4,731,000 in Selective Service administrative costs, it had been a grand bargain.[32]

Geographic Mobility

Although many young wives of conscientious objectors lived in their home communities working at jobs that provided some financial security, others moved closer to their husbands. Barbara Thomas, an Oklahoma Amish woman whose husband was drafted in 1942, stayed behind to harvest sixty acres of cotton; seven months later she followed her husband to Colorado, where he was working in CPS.[33]

Wives were not the only women who found their way to the camps. Some pacifist women sought to work alongside men in Civilian Public Service. In 1942 Louise Evans, a student at Vassar College, wrote to CPS officials that she wanted to spend her summer vacation helping conscientious objectors assigned to soil conservation projects near her parents' Colorado Springs home.[34] Manche Langley moved from Portland to Waldport, Oregon, where she rented a cabin near a CPS camp and designated herself Waldport's "USO girl." Camp administrators hired her as an assistant for their fine arts program; eventually, she learned to run the camp's printing press. One of Langley's contemporaries at Waldport described her as a kindred spirit among the camp's many artists and musicians, adding that she "enliven[ed] activities with her enthusiasms and outrageous comments."[35]

Across the country, in a suburb outside Washington, D.C., Elva Newswanger and her female housemates, all pacifists, liked to say that "we were running a USO [for men in the Beltsville, Maryland, unit]. . . . USO was a service organization for men in military service, and we felt we were doing a similar thing for CPS men." Newswanger, a Mennonite, had quit her secretarial job in the summer of 1941 after realizing that her firm, which manufactured bearings for machines, was stepping up contracts to produce parts for military equipment. At the invitation of a friend she moved from Pennsylvania to Washington to work for the National Service Board for Religious Objectors. "What interested me most," she recalled, "was that it was a program of the church, and I would be helping in a peace witness rather than the war effort."[36]

Civilian Public Service was full of lonely men eager for female companionship. Camps near colleges or universities were most likely to have female guests, sometimes in groups of twenty or more. Students from Smith College visited Camp Simon in New England for a weekend of dancing and socializing; students from Denison University spent a similar weekend at the camp near Coshocton, Ohio. Florida Southern College coeds dated C.O.s assigned to the unit at Mulberry, Florida. In Civilian Public Service settings across the country, C.O.s fell in love with local women who had had little or no previous exposure to pacifism. The results, predictably, were mixed. One man got a "Dear John" letter from

Civilian Public Service workers ice-skating at Terry, Montana, 1945.
(*Mennonite Library and Archives, Bethel College, North Newton, Kansas*)

a woman he had cared about deeply; she wrote that she didn't think she "could ever really become serious with a C.O."[37] Other women *did* get serious. At age seventeen, Betty Bragg met her future husband, a CPS assignee, when he began attending her church in Colorado Springs. "That was the first I had heard of C.O.s," she recalled later, "but I agreed with him."[38]

The stream of women appearing at base camps posed concerns for CPS leaders. Camp directors who dealt regularly with dependency problems and observed scores of visitors to the camps on Saturday afternoons and Sundays were ambivalent about the presence of assignees' wives. On the one hand, they wanted to accommodate married men who, they felt, might adjust better to CPS if their families lived nearby. But on the other hand, they concurred with the sentiment of one C.O. that "no girl should marry into this kind of life. It may sound like an adventure till you live it."[39]

Directors at base camps worried about the impact of women on camp life since some married men pooled rides into town to be with their wives until nine or ten P.M., depending on the camp curfew. During these absences men missed out on recreational and educational programs, including classroom and job training, which were designed to reinforce a sense of community. Camp directors also noticed that some engaged and married men were reluctant to volunteer for assignments that posed risks to personal safety or that required transfer to distant locations. As a

Civilian Public Service couples at a Saturday night dance, Trenton, North Dakota. (*Nancy Neumann, Maineville, Ohio*)

result, CPS officials brooded over what they perceived as the married men's "lack of freedom" to give themselves wholeheartedly to alternative service.[40]

In 1944 MCC officials arranged for Aganetha Fast, a former missionary to China, to travel for several months through western states visiting women who lived near Mennonite camps. An underlying rationale for her assignment was to guard camp morality. Mennonite Central Committee officials were sensitive to reports about breaches in conduct, such as unmarried sweethearts slipping away from base camps overnight. Fast, a pious woman some twenty years older than the generation of men and women in CPS, had little influence on the camp followers she encountered. Although she established several women's organizations — at Placerville, California, a "C.O. Club," and at Terry, Montana, the "Builderettes" — to strengthen relationships among women living near the camps, some viewed her as an intruder. At one gathering, Fast tried to dispel rumors that she had come to persuade the wives and friends of men in CPS to go home.[41]

Civilian Public Service policy during the war's early years prohibited married couples from living together in camp unless one or both were staff members. In 1941 a CPS official told a newlywed assigned to work near Colorado Springs that "we have eight married men in camp already and it would be impossible to start establishing quarters for the married people." He pointed out, however, that a few of the men in camp had found jobs and housing for their wives in town and added that "we certainly hope that it will not be long until these domestic disturbances cease, but until such time you will have to make the best of it as we are all trying to do."[42]

Some couples challenged this regulation. At a few small, out-of-the-way camps, wives lived with their C.O. husbands in open defiance. At larger camps, wives bent the rules by showering, laundering, and spending two or three nights a week in camp quarters while technically living elsewhere.[43] Most base camps remained under tighter discipline, however, and assignees without money, cars, or gasoline ration points found themselves isolated from their wives even when they were eligible for furloughs, which were accrued at two and a half days per month.

In 1942 the War Resisters League (WRL), a national antiwar organization whose members were especially critical of conscription, proposed that CPS officials reverse the ban on wives living with their husbands. After visiting twenty-three camps, WRL field secretary Frank Olmstead concluded that "the army seems to have a more charitable attitude" than the peace churches toward married conscripts.[44] Olmstead made several recommendations to Mennonite, Brethren, and Friends officials:

> Inasmuch as CPS men are allowed no wages it would seem only fair for the married men to have quarters within the camp grounds where they might live with their wives. The wives should be allowed the privilege of free board if they are not in a position to carry that expense for themselves. In cases where wives are unable to work through pregnancy or where small children are in the picture, it would seem that the very least the responsible authorities could do would be to adopt the minimum standards of the army in making financial provision for dependents.[45]

But historic peace church officials were reluctant to establish more generous living arrangements for C.O. families. The churches, they argued, simply could not afford to support camp followers. Some officials cited public relations as an even greater concern, noting that CPS was vulnerable to criticism that conscientious objectors lived in "luxury" while American soldiers died on distant battlefields. Leaders of the alternative service program had reason to be uneasy. At base camps where wives lived and worked only a few miles away, the intermittent presence of cars and women rankled local patriots. Even a party-line phone call placed by a wife to her C.O. husband at a nearby camp could inflame townspeople's emotions. In one community, members of the American Legion wrote to Selective Service officials, demanding to know whether women were permitted to "roam promiscuously" over CPS grounds.[46]

In mid-1943 Congressman W. Sterling Cole of New York investigated charges, made by constituents, that the AFSC camp at Big Flats, New York, was the site of a pacifist "lovenest."[47] After touring the camp, Cole complained to General Lewis B. Hershey that "the country respects the religious faith of any citizen in war as in peace, but this consideration should not extend to making available to conscientious objectors excessive privileges, opportunities and pleasures denied to men in military service."[48] But critics of the camp backed off after Lieutenant-Colonel Franklin A. McLean, a field inspector for Selective Service, visited Big Flats and reported that the camp director's wife supervised brief visits by wives and fiancées, who stayed in rooms at staff headquarters. According to McLean, the provisions made for female visitors to military bases were more generous than those available to CPS guests.[49]

After 1942, as growing numbers of married C.O.s were conscripted and Civilian Public Service expanded to include detached service — assignments in scientific research, farm work, and social work — CPS officials relaxed the ban on wives living with their husbands. Hundreds of men in CPS base camps requested transfers to locations closer to home or to newly opened units where their wives or friends could join them. On average, CPS assignees moved three times while in the program, filling newly established camps and units and accepting different kinds of work assignments.[50]

Wives who followed their husbands to CPS settings found work nearby as domestics, cooks, factory workers, clerks, secretaries, teachers, and child care workers. C.O.s assigned to work on dairy farms soon learned that their bosses *wanted* them to bring their wives along to do housework and tend livestock for wages ranging from twenty to fifty dollars a month. At mental hospital units, where labor shortages forced administrators to advertise job openings for women, C.O. wives who lived with their husbands and worked as ward attendants received an average salary of eighty dollars a month. Those qualified to work as nurses, lab technicians, or supervisors earned more. At a few locations the presence of C.O. wives reached a critical mass. In Marlboro, New Jersey, fifty-eight wives worked at the state mental hospital, and in Ypsilanti, Michigan, more than one hundred women joined the CPS community as mental hospital employees, volunteers, and members of a church-sponsored relief training unit.[51]

Children of Conscientious Objectors

Conscientious objectors who married during the war were generally hesitant to add to their financial burdens, and as a result, most delayed parenthood (see Table 3.2). C.O. wives worried that if they became pregnant they would have little choice but to move in with parents or other relatives. And like other women of their generation, many were reluctant to combine job and child rearing responsibilities; during the war, only one out of ten American mothers with children under the age of six entered the labor force.[52]

The use of contraceptives among married couples in CPS was widespread. During the war neither church nor government officials provided birth control counseling in any systematic way to conscientious objectors and their families, but couples in CPS settings were careful to avoid unwanted pregnancies. Married staff women who became pregnant were expected to leave camp by the fourth or fifth month, though some returned to work as soon as their infants were old enough to travel. At the Vineland Training School in New Jersey, an institution for the mentally retarded, school officials permitted married C.O. couples with work assignments to live together on the condition that if a wife became pregnant she would leave. Ruth Lehman, who joined her husband at the school, later recalled that "this happened to one of our number. The rest of us were *very* careful."[53] In Lyons, New Jersey, four C.O. wives moved into a farmhouse on the grounds of a mental hospital where their husbands had been assigned to work. For a brief time their husbands moved in, too, but a flurry of criticism in local newspapers prompted hospital officials to order the men to move back into dormitories. Thereafter, hospital authorities restricted the men to brief visits with their wives at the farmhouse, forbidding them even to enter the private quarters upstairs except to use the bathroom. One of the wives recalled: "Well, we abided by [the rules], believe me, and as a result I don't think there were any babies made at that time!"[54]

Nearly everyone in CPS knew of at least one couple for whom pregnancy had precipitated a financial or marital crisis. Assignees whose wives were pregnant tried to accumulate furlough time so that they might join

TABLE 3.2. Questionnaire and Oral History Respondents' Wartime Maternal Status

Dependent Children[a]	Number of Women	Percent of Sample
None	133	74
One	38	21
Two	8	4
Three	1	1
Total	180	100

[a]Includes children born prior to and during the war.

their families briefly after the birth, but few men received guarantees that they would be able to leave camp when they wished. Civilian Public Service camp directors, nurses, and matrons occasionally found themselves coordinating assistance for maternity cases. At the Fort Collins CPS camp, director John Schmidt urged an assignee whose pregnant wife was ill to take her to a doctor. The man replied, "I will, if she gets bad enough."[55] At the Trenton, North Dakota, camp an indigent mother moved into the CPS office with her newborn son after being evicted from a rental house in the nearby community of Williston. Though temporary, the arrangement frayed the nerves of everyone in camp. "We now have mama, baby, etc., right under foot," the Trenton dietitian wrote home. "The baby howls to high heaven, about ten hours a day."[56]

Many CPS wives with young children lived in their home communities, hundreds of miles away from their husbands. But others went to considerable lengths to keep their families together. In 1944 an Oregon woman who had just recovered from childbirth complications traveled by train with her daughters, ages two months and twenty months, to live near her husband's CPS camp in Montana. "That was a whole experience in itself," she recalled. "A cousin went with us. . . . We had shipped bedding, a few cooking utensils. Those were not disposable diaper days."[57]

During the war approximately one thousand children of conscientious objectors lived in or near Civilian Public Service sites. At camps where married staff members settled in with babies, toddlers, and preschoolers, male assignees welcomed and lavished attention on the children, who reminded them of their own. More typically, children lived with their mothers in communities a few miles from base camps or on the campuses of mental health institutions where CPS men were assigned

Chloe Goosen, age four, daughter of the cps camp director at North Fork, California, 1943. (*Cathryn Schmidt, Kansas City, Missouri*)

to work. Many families economized by sharing tourist cabins or apartments with others. Some wives working as live-in maids found quarters for themselves and their children in affluent homes. Others set up housekeeping in shelters that ranged from a chicken house on a Maryland farm, to a "New Hampshire ccc barracks with snow sifting across our bed during the winter," to "a cottage deep in the Florida woods, where [only] a few black neighbors may have known we were there as a family."[58]

In a few towns where colonies of cps camp followers developed, locals welcomed the women as a reliable source of labor. By January 1945, for example, forty wives of conscientious objectors had moved to Colorado Springs. The daily newspaper ran ads soliciting "Mennonite wives or ladies, with children or without, to work in private homes."[59] Similarly, toward the end of the war, officials at the state mental hospital in Marlboro, New Jersey, established a nursery on the hospital grounds for the children of cps couples and hired several C.O. wives to staff it. Hospital

Marlene Wiebe, daughter of CPS camp staff, in her playhouse near Hill City, South Dakota. (*Mennonite Library and Archives, Bethel College, North Newton, Kansas*)

administrators viewed the nursery as a temporary venture, expecting to close it as soon as conscientious objectors were demobilized. Twenty-nine children of C.O.s, ranging in age from a few months to three years, participated in this unique program. But ironically, their mothers rarely remained on the hospital payroll for more than a few months because they resented the grueling twelve-hour shifts that left them too little time with their children.[60]

For some wives, the most difficult aspect of wartime parenting involved the persecution of their children by other children. This disturbing consequence of parents' peace convictions affected even young children. Elsie Emmert, whose husband worked in CPS at Glacier National Park, related an incident involving her two-and-a-half-year-old son, Duane, in the nearby community of Kalispell: "One day some boys were playing out in front of our place, so he ran out to play with them. They picked up a rock and threw it at him and told him to go home, 'You little C.O.!' His head was cut quite badly. But our landlord went out and talked to the boys who threw the rock and told their parents. After that we didn't have any trouble."[61]

School-age children whose parents served on the staffs of Civilian Public Service camps faced almost certain harassment in classrooms and on playgrounds. As a result, families in CPS tried to determine whether

Tony Potts celebrating his fifth birthday in the CPS camp at Royalston, Massachusetts, with parents and friends. (*Florence Potts, Rifton, New York*)

or not schools in their vicinity were likely to safeguard their children's welfare. In Royalston, Massachusetts, Tom and Florence Potts, directors of an AFSC-sponsored camp, kept their six-year-old son, Tony, out of first grade because of concerns about the hostility he would face. Using a correspondence course, Florence Potts taught Tony in the family's camp quarters.[62]

All home front children who were old enough to know about the war were vulnerable to the fears of separation, violence, and even death that visited their generation. Children of conscientious objectors were as susceptible to anxiety as any, and, in addition, suffered cultural animosity directed at them and their parents.

Coping with Hostility

For hundreds of C.O. wives, World War II represented a period of cultural separation, and, in some cases, persecution. Among the Amish and among Mennonites who belonged to the more conservative branches of the church, plain dress functioned as a badge of nonresistance. But when the nation went to war, the attire could be cause for discomfort.

Families of conscientious objectors assigned to work at Marlboro State Hospital in New Jersey, 1945. (*Rose Yutzy, Elkhart, Indiana*)

In late 1941 the *Washington Evening Star* advised: "Smart women deck themselves with jewel-studded 'V' pins, 'V'-necked dresses, 'V'-hats and 'V'-bags."[63] By those standards women accustomed to living quiet lives in cultural noncompliance were not "smart" women. One who belonged to a Conservative Mennonite congregation recalled how conspicuous she felt "dressed like an Amish" when, on a trip to visit her husband in CPS camp, she boarded a train filled with soldiers on leave.[64]

For other wives, too, including those who embraced most aspects of American culture, the war offered somber lessons in nonconformity. Although they had been accustomed to mingling easily with coworkers and neighbors, their views on the war marked them as misfits. Both within and outside Civilian Public Service, women, more so than male C.O.s clustered in out-of-the-way camps, found themselves having to defend their stance to critics.[65] In extreme cases, local citizens were so hostile toward men in CPS camps that they threatened wives living in the area. Virginia Rohwer, who with other CPS wives worked in Manistee, Michigan, learned from sources at her husband's neighboring camp that "there was a movement among the town people to harm us," so she

Nursery for infants of conscientious objectors on the premises of Marlboro State Hospital, 1945. (*Ada Short, Archbold, Ohio*)

moved to the larger community of Grand Rapids, where she felt less vulnerable to hostility.[66] C.O. wives also left Henry, Illinois, after hostile locals threatened to "go up the river" to the CPS camp and "wipe out the C.O.s." At the height of the crisis, Daniel Yutzy, a CPS assignee and cook at the Henry camp, urged his wife, Rose, to get out of town, and within hours she was on her way back to her home community of Middlebury, Indiana, "worrying every mile of the way."[67]

Civilian Public Service units located on the grounds of mental hospitals and training schools, which attracted large numbers of C.O. wives, faced difficulties when regular employees mistreated C.O. workers. At the Mansfield State Hospital for the Mentally Retarded and Epileptics in Connecticut, C.O.s attributed their strained relations with employees to general antipathy toward pacifistic beliefs and to unfounded fears that members of the CPS unit wanted to keep their jobs after the war. Although C.O. wives who joined the Mansfield staff were entitled to the same employment provisions as regular employees, they sometimes bore the brunt of workplace hostility. One C.O. wife, a switchboard operator, recalled that her supervisor expressed daily "her hatred for the C.O.s and their wives."[68]

Some wives escaped harassment entirely. Women who lived in cities,

Eloise Zabel, spouse of a CPS assignee, serving food in the women's section of Marlboro State Hospital in New Jersey, 1946. (*Mennonite Library and Archives, Bethel College, North Newton, Kansas*)

unlike those in smaller communities, enjoyed a cloak of anonymity that protected them from scrutiny. Likewise, women who worked on family farms or in church-related jobs were sheltered from the pressures felt by women who taught school or worked in other high-profile occupations. Those who found themselves in uncomfortable positions with coworkers tried to draw on reservoirs of goodwill from long-established relationships. Mary Morgan was teaching in her hometown of Eddystone, Pennsylvania, when her husband left for an Ohio camp. In 1942 Morgan learned that she and other teachers would be expected to issue ration booklets and register men for the draft. She refused the registration assignment, reasoning that "I should not send men to the war while I was a C.O." Although her refusal cost her a day's pay, her fellow teachers, who had known her for years, took the incident in stride.[69]

Most women whose husbands or fiancés were in Civilian Public Service made no attempt to hide that information from bosses or coworkers. Verda De Coursey, who worked in an office in Utah, recalled that coworkers did not understand her position, but neither were they antagonistic. In assessing her work relationships, De Coursey commented: "I tended not to flaunt our pacifism, but I did not deny it."[70] Like De Coursey, most women associated with CPS found that coworkers were tolerant of their views. Some wives discovered that explaining the provisions of Civilian Public Service helped to dispel tension. Critics were often surprised to learn, for example, that the men assigned to CPS worked without pay.

But a smaller number of women who felt vulnerable tried to protect their identity. In Minnesota, Ruby Moody, who during the interwar period had been a peace activist, found that her circumstances changed dramatically after she married a CPS man and became pregnant. She arranged for her child to be delivered in a charity ward and lived as frugally as possible in a rented room. Not wishing to risk eviction, she vaguely told her landlord and anyone else who asked that her husband worked "for the government out West." Her story had an ironic twist. Months later, after her landlord died, Moody was stunned to read in his obituary that he had been a conscientious objector in the First World War.[71]

Some women learned to hide personal information after experiencing the pain of job or housing discrimination. In 1945 Virginia Krehbiel, who worked as a bookkeeper in a Kansas grocery store, became engaged to a man in CPS and promptly lost her job. Her boss told her that he hated to do it but explained that the head butcher, who had a son in the navy, was demanding that she be fired. Several months later, Krehbiel married and moved to Nebraska, where she took a job as a clerk in a large grocery chain. She was careful not to include on her application any information identifying her with the local CPS unit. When asked about her husband, she replied simply: "He's working." But before long her new coworkers learned of her husband's stance, and she was devastated to lose the second job as well.[72]

Job discrimination against C.O. women on the American home front occurred routinely. In some kinds of work, they faced policies that applied to other women as well. School boards, for example, often refused to hire married women. Prior to the war, nearly six in ten American communities followed this policy; a decade later, only 8 percent were persisting in the practice.[73] In addition to this general form of job discrimination, C.O. women faced unique obstacles in trying to support themselves financially. In 1942 the wife of a CPS man described in a letter to her husband an interview with an Ohio school superintendent:

> He asked me many questions until finally, 'What does your husband do?' And immediately on hearing that you were at camp he said he couldn't use me. He can't understand the philosophy behind men *going* to such a camp: he believes that peace groups have gotten us into this trouble — kept us from being prepared; . . . that people who believe as we do should go to another country and set up a community of their own, . . . that we still have free speech here — too much — otherwise we'd have been prepared. He fought in the last war — volunteered to join the army.

> He was calm and quiet throughout, and did allow me to answer his statements — which I did as well as I could. He ended by writing 'C.O.' in the corner of my application and saying that he believed we probably thought alike about many things but that our basic philosophy on this subject was entirely different (as it certainly is).[74]

She concluded: "It might be necessary or wise to seek the anonymity of a large city system, but of course even there, the superintendent might have the same reaction."[75]

Women who were fired or were denied employment on the basis of their beliefs had no recourse but to try to find work from more sympathetic employers. Most managed to do so but paid the price of downward occupational mobility. A number of C.O. wives who worked as domestics during the war later reported that they found the low-paying work available in private homes preferable to the harassment they had experienced previously in business or industry.[76]

Because of federal policies that discriminated against conscientious objectors, including the denial of family allotments, the wives and children of C.O.s bore particular hardships. Since spouses of men in Civilian Public Service were responsible for supporting themselves, bread-and-butter issues of housing, employment, and child care dominated their lives. Most who moved to be near their husbands found that they managed reasonably well as long as they remained in good health and could turn to like-minded women for friendship and assistance. For a CPS family arriving in an unfamiliar community, the presence of other wives and children had countless benefits. Women shared tips on job openings, arranged for cooperative child care, took turns cooking evening meals, socialized, and traveled together. Especially in times of health or financial crisis, these networks of C.O. friends were significant sources of support.[77]

Ultimately, CPS camp followers would offer mixed assessments of alternative service. A woman who spent several years living in poverty with her children at the edge of her husband's camp in Montana recalled, "CPS was a very important part of our lives. It was a very hard part but a very good part . . . [in] knowing we had done the right thing."[78] Like the majority of women who had followed men to Civilian Public Service settings, she had lived in the margins of a society that provided legal sanction for conscientious objection but had little patience for it.

4 Looking for a Few Good Women

FREE
Conscientious
Objectors
from
U.S. prisons

For dietitians and nurses across America the war offered new and welcome prospects for travel and adventure. From 1941 on, women in these professions who had pacifist convictions discovered that Civilian Public Service work held a similar allure. In the fall of 1944 Naomi Brubaker, a Pennsylvanian and recent college graduate, was waiting for an assignment as CPS dietitian when a Mennonite Central Committee official told her of four camp openings: two in California, one in Montana, and one in Colorado. Brubaker, who had never been west of Indiana, responded: "Well, if I'm getting a free ride, I'll go the furthest. . . . Might as well go to California!"[1]

Of the approximately two thousand women who lived in and near Civilian Public Service camps, an estimated 15 percent had official duties as paid staff members.[2] Women were present especially at large base camps of a hundred or more men, where dietitians supervised kitchen crews and nurses ran infirmaries. At many of these locations, camp directors' or business managers' wives—often known as matrons—assumed hosting responsibilities.

These CPS staff women performed a unique function in wartime, even though the broader patterns of their lives intersected with those of millions of other American women engaged in various forms of voluntarism and paid labor. Nurses and dietitians in CPS were among the growing number of American women who were employed outside the home during the war. By 1944 gainfully employed women constituted one-third of the U.S. work force.[3] Yet while the Roosevelt administration launched promotional campaigns to entice women into military or industrial work, those who signed on with Civilian Public Service were interested in pursuing service-oriented vocations among conscientious objectors.

A crucial difference in the experiences of CPS men and women was that, despite intermittent threats of universal conscription, women never had to face the draft. Because draft legislation did not apply to them, what they did was of their own choosing. The nurses, matrons, and dietitians who entered CPS did so under fundamentally different conditions than did men. One dietitian later recalled that in CPS she never felt exactly like a participant since men in base camps often teased: "You can leave!"[4] Women in CPS spent far less time than men justifying to themselves or others their decision to participate in alternative service. For the most part, they liked what they were doing and consequently were less prone than drafted C.O.s to burdens of frustration and guilt.

Civilian Public Service staff women were, at least superficially, a more homogeneous group than the male C.O.s with whom they lived and worked. The women were relatively young; most came into CPS while they were in their twenties. As a group they were also well educated. Nearly all of the nurses held graduate degrees from nursing schools, and perhaps half the dietitians had had college-level training in home economics. Most came from Mennonite, Brethren, or Quaker backgrounds and enjoyed the support of their families, although some entered Civilian Public Service despite the disapproval of relatives who did not share a commitment to pacifism.[5]

Historian Barbara J. Steinson contends that during the First World War, American women peace activists pursued new opportunities outside the domestic sphere while simultaneously embracing the ideal of a "nurturant motherhood." This ideology was attractive to World War I era pacifists because it enabled them to claim traditional values of home and family even as they boldly questioned public policy. Their emphasis on femininity provided a rationalization for their participation in activities that lay beyond the pale of traditional women's work.[6]

Amy Swerdlow, in her study of the Women Strike for Peace movement, argues that during the 1950s and 1960s similar dynamics of women's culture were at play in the lives of antinuclear activists. In Women Strike for Peace, which was composed largely of homemakers and mothers, members forged a sense of identity from both traditional gender ideology *and* collective action as peacemakers.[7] Steinson's and Swerdlow's descriptions of American women peace activists prior to and following World War II resemble those of the women who aligned themselves with conscientious objectors in Civilian Public Service. Yet the milieu into which CPS staff women immersed themselves was unquestionably a male culture.

The skewed gender ratio of Civilian Public Service camps cast staff women into prominence as surrogate mothers or sisters. Their assignments as organizers, preparers of food, health care givers, decorators, and providers of hospitality were commonplace sources of feminine identity. Marie Lohrenz, a single Mennonite woman from Minnesota, was in her early forties when she became staff nurse for a CPS base camp with several hundred men. Though she had been reluctant to take the assignment, she found that the work was both demanding and satisfying: "I figured I had been in the best one," she later recalled. "The men always called me 'Mom'; they'd say, 'Hi, Mom!' I let them — what of it? I *did* play like a mom to them — the young ones felt lonely."[8] Most CPS staff women, ten or fifteen years younger than Lohrenz, would have vehemently resisted the maternal label. Yet they too found in their work settings a pervasive and relaxed familiarity. Gender roles in camp settings were conventional, and staff women slipped easily into the positions expected of them.

Recruiting Staff Members

Both "push" and "pull" factors influenced women to spend the war years in, as one AFSC official put it, "hard work on a semi-service basis."[9] The program had obvious enticements for women strongly opposed to the war, or whose husbands or fiancés were already in camp. Nurses, dietitians, and matrons assigned to CPS camps usually worked for salaries ranging from twenty-five to forty dollars per month, plus room, board, and medical care. Most women on staff also received two weeks or more of vacation per year, although gas and tire rationing restricted travel. After 1942, as Civilian Public Service expanded and new units opened at mental hospitals, more women joined the program as aides, dietitians, nurses, and administrative staff. At mental hospitals women could earn higher wages: sixty to one hundred dollars a month for jobs on the wards, more for nursing supervisors and other professionals.[10]

On the other hand, a few women were "pushed" to take part in Civilian Public Service because of home front realities that limited their employment options. Frequently, professional women who opposed the war experienced downward occupational mobility. During the early 1940s some C.O. teachers lost or left their jobs because school boards or administrators would not tolerate their views. These women saw CPS as a means to support themselves after experiencing painful conflicts in other work settings.[11]

For some women professionals, the chance to contribute to Civilian Public Service more than compensated for the pressure to advance their careers in more acceptable civilian or military settings. In the spring of 1942 Mary Emma Showalter, a Mennonite, was completing a bachelor's degree in home economics at Madison College when she informed her adviser that she planned to accept a position as dietitian at a CPS camp in Virginia. The professor admonished: "What do you mean, after four years of preparation, to bury yourself in such work on some mountainside? Your men had better go to war and help defend their country instead of being cowards." Showalter responded: "If you are calling those men cowards then call me one too because they are my brothers and cousins and friends."[12] Showalter began her work a month later and remained a CPS dietitian and consultant for Mennonite Central Committee throughout the war.

Civilian Public Service officials had difficulty finding qualified dietitians since their services were in demand on military bases and in hospitals at home and abroad. Administrators for the American Friends Service Committee recruited heavily among women who in the past decade had participated in AFSC work camps, the Quakers' summer service program for young adults.[13] Mennonite Central Committee leaders kept in close contact with Mennonite college administrators, who referred them to home economics graduates as potential CPS dietitians. Although MCC tried to hire trained dietitians, women who arrived at camps came from a variety of backgrounds. At some locations, wives of camp directors or other camp staff fell into these jobs regardless of training or preparation. One woman who had a young daughter to care for but nonetheless was pressed to service in her husband's camp remembered that "it was hard to be creative with limited resources. . . . The men who did the cooking probably knew more than I did."[14]

Beginning in 1943, the AFSC, BSC, and MCC addressed the shortage of qualified dietitians by establishing a number of "CPS cooking schools." At a dozen locations across the country, groups of ten to thirty male CPS assignees came together for instruction by professional dietitians. These courses, patterned after hotel management programs and the U.S. Army's schools for cooks and bakers, combined principles of nutrition with food preparation techniques.[15] At each cooking school, stu-

Civilian Public Service cooking school and kitchen crew at North Fork, California, 1943. (*Mennonite Library and Archives, Bethel College, North Newton, Kansas*)

dents prepared meals for a local CPS camp. After completing the course, cooks received certificates from their sponsoring agency and assumed new responsibilities in CPS camps or units. Later, after the war had ended, some of these specially trained cooks accepted overseas assignments for relief and rehabilitation work.

Civilian Public Service recruiters faced even greater problems finding staff nurses, in part because of powerful cultural expectations that young, physically able nurses should enlist in the armed forces. Throughout World War II American nurses who thought of themselves as C.O.s worried that they might be pressed into military service. Some signed on with the American Red Cross, even though historic peace church leaders warned that in times of international conflict, the agency "becomes inseparably linked with the war . . . and becomes a vastly different organization from its peacetime humanitarian service."[16]

In 1942 the responsibility for filling quotas for military nursing needs shifted from the Red Cross to the nursing profession, and a number of state and local nursing councils began promoting compulsory registration of all nurses. But since women were not subject to the Selective Training and Service Act that conscripted men, the nursing councils had to rely on moral suasion. The councils launched a national campaign to bring nurses out of retirement by broadcasting the Red Cross's urgent needs through radio announcements, women's magazines, professional journals, and churches. But as better paying jobs became available to women in defense industries and elsewhere, the responses of inactive nurses to these appeals were disappointing. So while the Red Cross continued to certify nurses, government and nursing officials collaborated on a legislative solution — "universal conscription" — to address the military nursing shortage.[17]

Key advisers to President Roosevelt, including Eleanor Roosevelt, advocated the voluntary registration of women between the ages of eighteen and sixty-five. In 1942 and 1943 Congress debated three universal conscription measures, known as the Baldwin bill, the Bilbo bill, and the Austin-Wadsworth bill. A Gallup poll conducted in September 1943 indicated that 81 percent of Americans thought that single women should be drafted for noncombatant military service before more fathers were taken. Seventy-five percent of single women themselves endorsed this proposal. Reluctantly the American Nurses' Association and other nursing organizations lent support to proposals for women's conscription on the grounds that if enough nurses did not volunteer for military duty, they should be drafted.[18] Yet despite the mobilization of support for universal conscription, labor, peace, and feminist groups organized significant opposition to it, and most members of Congress remained unconvinced that conscripting women was necessary or desirable.

Throughout the long debate over universal conscription C.O. nurses and nursing students wondered nervously about their future. During the summer of 1942 MCC official Albert Gaeddert reported that several nursing school graduates had gone before their state examining board and learned that they would not be issued certificates of registration unless they volunteered to serve in the armed forces.[19] That fall, a Mennonite woman wrote to CPS officials:

> I am a graduate nurse and am interested in some type of nursing in place of army nursing. I believe that my peace principles could be carried out more effectively outside the army or navy.
>
> I have delayed writing because help is needed here at the Mennonite Hospital [in Bloomington, Illinois], but according to a recent Red Cross meeting, we will be taken regardless, if we are not a supervisor or head nurse.

Since I will not be permitted to help here much longer I feel that I should make an effort to find some type of nursing where I can still carry out our principle of peace. Someone told me that there are C.O. camp nurses. Is there room for any more nurses in the camps? Or are there also other ways in which we can serve?[20]

Some nurses who wanted to free themselves from hospital work ran into resistance from the Roosevelt administration's War Manpower Commission, which closely monitored employment at American hospitals. Despite the threat that nurses would be "frozen" in their jobs, CPS officials placed volunteer nurses into camps whenever possible. But even women who accepted such posts could not feel secure about their future, and the church agencies responsible for CPS worried that bureaucratic snags—such as the failure of nurses to obtain registration in the states where they had been assigned—would further jeopardize their status.[21]

In 1942 and 1943 Civilian Public Service assignees joined many other Americans in anxiously following congressional debates over universal conscription. At some camps, C.O.s embarked on letter-writing campaigns to urge elected officials not to draft women. Others in CPS sent money and letters of encouragement to the National Committee to Oppose the Conscription of Women, a group directed by prominent Friend and women's rights advocate Mildred Scott Olmsted.[22]

As prospects for universal conscription began to dim, Congress considered an emergency measure known as the Bolton Act, named for Ohio congresswoman Frances Payne Bolton. Passed in June 1943, this act established the U.S. Cadet Nurse Corps and made free nursing education available to students willing to commit themselves to military or civilian national service. Thus the Roosevelt administration had a new tool for enlisting nurses. By the end of the war nearly half of the 240,000 active registered nurses in the country, many of whom did not meet the military's physical requirements, had volunteered.[23] Ultimately, none of the proposals for drafting women evolved into law because so many American women volunteered as nurses and as WACs, WAVES, SPARs, and marines.

Although the Public Health Service—not Selective Service—administered the Cadet Nurse Corps, peace church denominations viewed the corps as a paramilitary organization. Neither the Friends nor the Brethren operated nursing schools during the war years, but the three Ameri-

The U.S. Army Nurse Corps. (*National Archives, College Park, Maryland*)

can Mennonite nursing schools, affiliated with hospitals in Illinois, Kansas, and Colorado, chose not to participate in the Cadet Nurse Corps program or accept federal funds. By retaining such an independent stance Mennonite officials were able to recruit more effectively among their own young people for CPS or relief work. As late as mid-1945, for example, representatives of the Mennonite Central Committee were contacting Mennonite nursing students and urging them to "give a year or two of service" to CPS in lieu of military duty.[24]

The historic peace church agencies faced a large task in finding enough women to staff the expanding CPS program. Shortages of nurses and dietitians were particularly serious in Quaker-run camps. Friends comprised only about 8 percent of the men assigned to CPS, and because their numbers were so small, AFSC leaders had trouble recruiting Quaker women to fill positions. In 1944 Arthur Gamble, the AFSC's business manager, declared that "hearing about a stray nurse who might be available for CPS makes me feel like a gold miner in the year 1849."[25]

In desperation, AFSC administrators considered trying to secure the release of Japanese American nurses, doctors, and dentists from internment camps for rotation in CPS, but Selective Service officials replied that Japanese American nurses, already working in internment camps, were unavailable for CPS work.[26] The AFSC then sent representatives to various regions of the country to try to persuade registered nurses to leave their jobs for CPS. But by early 1944 a senior AFSC official concluded that "the process of seeking them out and shaking them loose from private practice is very difficult," and with reluctance the AFSC arranged for male assignees to serve as infirmary attendants in some of its camps.[27]

Although officials of the Mennonite Central Committee relied occasionally on male infirmary attendants, the MCC was more successful in persuading qualified nurses to work in Civilian Public Service. This was due largely to the emergence of the Mennonite Nurses' Association (MNA), the first professional organization for Mennonite women. The MNA's founders, Maude Swartzendruber and Verna Zimmerman, both staff members of a Mennonite-affiliated nursing school in LaJunta, Colorado, hoped to emphasize nursing as an act of Christian service. Ironically, one of their chief goals was to counteract what they perceived as the secularization of their profession.[28]

In 1941 concerned about impending pressures on nurses, Swartzendruber and Zimmerman began to plan an organization that they hoped would shore up the church's longstanding prohibition against participation in war. These women sought to counter military recruitment efforts by educating Mennonite nurses and nursing students about career alternatives. Swartzendruber, Zimmerman, and their colleagues believed that the few Mennonite nurses already known to have enlisted in the armed forces probably lacked information about the church's emphasis on alternative service since church-based draft counseling had been aimed primarily at men.[29]

In 1942 the women drew up a constitution declaring their intent to "formulate a program for Mennonite nurses as conscientious objectors during a wartime crisis."[30] To solicit members, the MNA publicized its existence via letters to Mennonite bishops and ministers throughout the United States and Canada. After establishing a binational membership and chapters in Ontario, Iowa, Colorado, Pennsylvania, Virginia, Kansas, and Indiana, the Mennonite Nurses' Association sent questionnaires to its members to assist MCC in placing qualified women in Civilian Public Service camps and overseas relief work.[31]

The nurses' successful organizational efforts belie the barriers they overcame in working through Mennonite church structures. Although the founders of the MNA were eager to develop the nursing association on their own terms, they faced the possibility of censure by their denomination's male leadership. Throughout the 1910s, 1920s, and 1930s members of the conservative Mennonite Church denomination, also known as the (old) Mennonites, had struggled over gender issues, from the right of women to speak in public meetings to proscribed dress. Many women among the (old) Mennonites, for example, wore head coverings to indicate women's submission to men. Verna Zimmerman, Maude Swartzendruber, and their nursing colleagues, all members of the Mennonite Church, were certain that the formation of a new women's organization would stir churchwide opposition. But as Zimmerman later explained, "We felt that nursing was so removed from what the men were doing. We wanted to run our own show."[32]

In essence, they did. In their constitution, the nurses made provision for an ordained minister to serve as an "adviser" to the organization. Disingenuously, Zimmerman invited Sanford Yoder, secretary of the (old) Mennonites' mission board, to serve in this position. Yoder, whom the women considered a friend and advocate, agreed, and the arrangement worked well, for male denominational leaders never obstructed the Mennonite nurses' efforts to develop an autonomous organization.[33]

Throughout World War II the possibility that American nurses might be drafted shaped the agenda of the Mennonite Nurses' Association. Renewed threats came in early January 1945 when President Roosevelt, in his State of the Union address, projected critical shortages in the army and called for the drafting of nurses. A month later, two Gallup polls showed that most Americans supported drafting single nurses between the ages of twenty and forty-five.[34] Again, C.O. nurses came under strong pressure to enlist.

Responding to these calls, the Mennonite Nurses' Association carried in their monthly publication an essay by Harold S. Bender, a prominent Mennonite educator. Bender, commenting on the divisiveness in Mennonite communities over the role of professional women in wartime, said that he had been "shocked in the last war to discover that there were some people who thought that because a nurse's ministry is healing and helping the sick she could enter into the armed forces with a good conscience, even a Christian nonresistant nurse."[35] Bender shared the view of many religious pacifists that the federal government should make provision for civilian service for nurses who conscientiously opposed war.

From January through March 1945 Congress considered three newly proposed bills to conscript nurses. But by the spring of 1945, Allied military victories in Europe signaled that the war would soon end, and the politically charged issue of drafting nurses dissipated. As a result, Congress never considered the idea that nurses be offered conscientious objector status.[36]

Matrons and Nurses

The church agency officials who recruited women into CPS believed that staff women would play an important role in boosting the morale of conscientious objectors.[37] Given the uncertainties of war, it seemed a truism that the mere presence of women could add a civilizing touch to the mostly male camps. An early article in the secular press about CPS noted: "To keep a community of men from falling into slothful ways, each camp has two women on the staff. . . . CCC [Civilian Conservation Corps] barrack buildings have become 'dormitories' and are freshly decorated. Flowers grow in window boxes."[38]

In CPS locations across the United States staff women established routines that combined professional duties with the expectation that they would lend a "woman's hand" to the overall life of the camp.[39] A "dietitians' handbook" written for CPS staff suggested that as "one of the few women in camp, your duties are not limited to the confines of the kitchen."[40] In most MCC-affiliated camps administrators designated one woman as matron. AFSC- and BSC-sponsored camps, however, placed less emphasis on communal behavior and did not have regular matrons, although camp directors' wives sometimes assumed the role unofficially.

In Mennonite camps the matron was usually the wife of a camp staffer. Officials who recruited matrons examined candidates' "experience and education, ability to work with young men and win their respect and cooperation, . . . and ability to carry the spirit of the home and an atmosphere of refinement and culture into the camp."[41] The women who accepted positions as matrons often hosted guests, supervised assignees in laundering and ironing clothes, inspected dormitories for orderliness, and oversaw the camp library. In general, matrons acted as housemothers to the resident C.O.s.[42]

Nurses' duties overlapped considerably with the work of matrons, and in some of the smaller camps, solitary staff women performed both roles. Civilian Public Service nurses were expected to verify the illnesses of

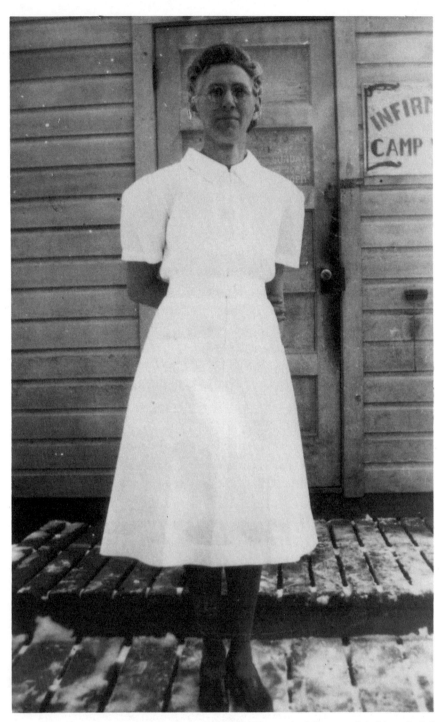

Mary Duerksen, CPS nurse at Lapine, Oregon. (*Mennonite Library and Archives, Bethel College, North Newton, Kansas*)

Edna Peters, CPS nurse at Hill City, South Dakota. (*Mennonite Central Committee Photograph Collection, IX-13-2, Archives of the Mennonite Church, Goshen, Indiana*)

men who claimed to be too sick to work. They also cared for patients in the camp infirmary, provided first aid, inspected camp facilities for proper sanitation, and served as liaison between patients, family members, doctors, and hospital officials.[43]

Early in the war, the church agencies administering CPS drew up policies outlining coverage of medical care for assignees, staff members, and their families. They made arrangements with local doctors to be on call and to make periodic visits to the camps. Civilian Pubic Service officials did their best to locate physicians within driving distance who were likely to maintain cordial relations with the conscientious objectors. But when CPS directors were unable to recruit sympathetic doctors, even greater responsibility fell to staff nurses to provide preventive care, diagnosis, and medical treatment.[44]

Occasionally, CPS staff women provided a broader range of care than they had anticipated. One nurse went beyond the call of duty while serving at a reclamation camp near Hill City, South Dakota. From time to time, when someone living in the Black Hills had an accident or was ill, people came looking for her at the camp infirmary. She made house calls free of charge and later commented: "Some of the neighbors who lived around the camp weren't the friendliest to our boys, but they knew where to come when they were sick."[45]

The duties of a CPS nurse depended on the size and location of the camp, the nature of the work performed by the men, and the degree to which assignees cooperated with CPS authorities. Where camp relationships were relatively smooth and morale high, the work of the nurse was routine: keeping medical supplies in stock, administering smallpox and typhoid vaccines, caring for the injured and ill, and recording all visits to the infirmary.

Sometimes the routine was broken by serious illness or accident, or even death. Thirty men died while in Civilian Public Service, some while on hazardous work assignments, some as a result of non-work-related injuries, and some of natural causes. When death occurred, the camp staff, and particularly the nurse or matron, counseled bereaved parents and friends. Occasionally, camp life was disrupted by mentally ill assignees who ought not have been inducted into alternative service or who could not adjust to the routines of CPS. In these cases, camp directors or nurses tried to arrange for medical discharge.[46]

Nurses found that the camps they served varied not only in the idiosyncrasies of particular assignees, but also in the level of well-being or malaise that permeated the entire community. Catherine Harder began her CPS nursing career in Missoula, Montana, working among a select group of conscientious objectors assigned to be smoke jumpers for the U.S. Forest Service. Although their physical training was strenuous and resulted in many injuries, the nurse noticed that men in her infirmary were eager to get back into training. Her next CPS assignment was among men whose daily work was much more tedious. At this second camp, Harder discovered "some malingering," for which she was unprepared. Dealing with malingerers, or what CPS staffers called "goldbrickers," proved to be an occupational hazard for most camp nurses. Some tried to cut down the length of the daily sick list, insisting that the men they

Smoke jumpers in Civilian Public Service at Missoula, Montana, practicing under the direction of the U.S. Forest Service. A jump from the training tower simulates jumping from a plane. (*American Friends Service Committee, Civilian Public Service, Swarthmore College Peace Collection, Swarthmore, Pennsylvania*)

suspected of faking or exaggerating illness report to work. Nurses battled the feeling that chronic complainers were taking advantage of them and tried to develop a thick skin in dealing with men who frequented the infirmary.[47]

As part of a staff team that normally included a director, assistant director, business manager, dietitian, and education director, CPS nurses worked in collaboration with others. Yet the relative isolation of most camp settings also encouraged nurses to work autonomously. For example, each of the church agencies instructed staff nurses to keep a professional appearance by wearing uniforms. But the rule was rarely enforced, and in most camps, nurses chose more casual dress. Staff women did not regard uniforms as paramilitary dress but, as in other work-related matters, wanted to rely on their own judgment in choosing practical clothes that required a minimum of care.[48]

Throughout the war most CPS nurses felt that they played a vital role in camp life and found their experiences both challenging and satisfying. When serious medical emergencies arose, they made sure that a physician took charge. But most of the time camp nurses handled problems independently. One Mennonite nurse recalled her pride in feeling that in CPS she had been "the doctor as well as the nurse."[49]

Dietitians in Civilian Public Service

Like nurses, dietitians recruited to work among conscientious objectors were responsible for well-defined tasks. The church agencies expected dietitians at most CPS base camps to order food, deal with wholesalers and ration boards, keep records of purchases, plan meals, train kitchen workers, and organize the kitchen crew in a rotation for food preparation, service, and clean-up. Less typically, some women hired on as dietitians at hospitals where CPS men were assigned to work. Lillian Pemberton Willoughby, the wife of a conscientious objector, worked for eighteen months as head dietitian at Alexian Brothers Hospital in Chicago and earned two hundred dollars a month. On that relatively high salary, Willoughby supported her family of three and was able to pay another CPS wife for on-site child care.[50]

Creativity and improvisational skills were essential qualifications for dietitians at base camps. This was particularly true for those who joined CPS early in the war and had to establish kitchens from scratch. In the fall of 1940 Nancy Foster, a Swarthmore-educated schoolteacher from Ohio, negotiated release from her employment contract and joined the fledgling Civilian Public Service program. Foster came to her new position well prepared, for during the 1930s she had volunteered as a cook for AFSC summer work camps. In February 1941, after arriving in Baltimore where she and fellow AFSC workers planned to establish the first camp for conscientious objectors, she wrote her parents:

We are supposed to have a camp at Patapsco State Forest, ten miles south of town, but there seem to be various hitches, mostly connected with the government. In the first place, the camp is an awful mess, with very unsatisfactory sanitary facilities. In the second there is absolutely no equipment. . . . Rumors of great interest circulate constantly:

'The government will provide everything — stoves to can openers.'

'The government will provide beds, stoves, basic kitchen equipment, and AFSC will provide the rest.'

'The government is very desperate for equipment for the army and will provide nothing.'[51]

Foster concluded dryly, "Meanwhile, here we sit"; but during the next two months she and her colleagues managed to open the Patapsco camp. For the next four years, Foster worked as a dietitian in five camps from New England to the Great Plains. Civilian Public Service, in her view, had much to commend it, including "wonderful people, new places and experiences, the honing of skills which stood me in good stead for relief work and living in the backwoods of Mexico, and a broader understanding of religion and life in general."[52] But just as vividly, she remembered the difficulties she encountered in CPS. In 1944 Foster wrote of her frustrations:

Doing nothing for one's self, in a way — having food appear on the table three times a day without paying any board bill, getting clothes from the storeroom and reclaiming them from our very communal laundry, trading haircuts, having even the newspaper provided for one, handling the cash money that a grade school child might handle — what effect is that going to have on adults after a long enough period of time? Of course, the army is in many ways the same. . . . [Soldiers] lead an even more artificial and irresponsible existence. That's why conscription is so terrible, in that it makes such a life legal and binding on so many human beings.

And yet, when I see the difficulties we get into . . . the rampant selfishness and occasional intolerance here, I wonder how a world will ever evolve free of wars and hatred.[53]

Without exception, dietitians in Civilian Public Service became sensitive to the problem of trying to maintain harmony among a heterogeneous population of conscientious objectors. Depending on the camp, the men they supervised in the kitchen could be even more fractious than the CPS men assigned to daily work crews. Foster noticed that kitchen workers often included a "problem child" and other assignees who government supervisors did not want to oversee.[54]

Beginning in 1942, the church agencies chose a few experienced dietitians to travel to CPS locations across the country to serve as consultants to camp staff. During the next several years the Mennonite Central Committee also recruited a few women to visit CPS camps as instructors in music and crafts, expecting that these activities would help to alleviate the stress and boredom of camp life. One of the women who traveled on behalf of MCC later recalled that while she had spent much of her time helping on-site dietitians solve problems related to budget constraints, her visits were also meant to "convey the message to the women on staff that MCC recognized their assignments as difficult and often lonely."[55]

Staff women sometimes faced problems with fellow workers. At one camp, a male business manager and female dietitian had chronic difficulty staying within their food budget. The consulting dietitian who visited the camp found that the business manager did not permit his female colleague to meet with food salesmen who came around or participate in decisions about purchases. In such cases, the consulting dietitian was to serve as an advocate for staff members, alerting CPS administrators to interpersonal problems.[56]

Meal planning also tested the ingenuity of CPS dietitians. Dietitians were responsible for providing a variety of foods to large groups of men whose individual tastes ran the gamut from particular ethnic cuisines, such as Pennsylvania Dutch cooking, to vegetarianism. Some C.O.s avoided meat or dairy products because of religious or philosophical principles, but more commonly, one dietitian recalled, assignees "were accustomed to having good, hefty farm meals two or three times a day" and yearned for meat, eggs, milk, cream, and fresh produce.[57] In lieu of these foods CPS dietitians used large amounts of beans, peanut butter, and locally available foods. One dietitian assigned to a California base camp was delighted with the exotic produce donated by area farmers, including mangoes, avocados, and Persian melons. At a Massachusetts camp, some C.O.s regularly fasted on Friday nights and sent the savings in meal costs to the AFSC for war relief work. The fast was moderately popular because on those evenings many men picked and ate wild blueberries, and on Saturdays the camp dietitian made pies with the leftovers as "a little bonus for the fast."[58]

As the war stretched from months to years, food shortages posed new

Food supply at the CPS camp in Terry, Montana, 1945.
(*Mennonite Library and Archives, Bethel College, North Newton, Kansas*)

challenges for Civilian Public Service dietitians. The scarcity of rural workers to tend six million farms nationwide signaled a crisis for the Roosevelt administration. In September 1942 U.S. Secretary of Agriculture Claude Wickard testified before the House Committee on Agriculture: "Unless we can find some way to deal with the farm labor problem and other problems of farm production satisfactorily, we must find some way, in the not too distant future, to deal with a shortage of food. Food is just as much a weapon in this war as guns."[59] Federal officials recognized the acute need for agricultural workers and found new sources of labor among imported foreign workers from Mexico and elsewhere, prisoners of war, Japanese Americans on furlough from relocation centers, conscientious objectors in CPS, and American-based servicemen. In addition, the government created a Victory Farm Volunteers program for 2.5 million youths, ages fourteen to seventeen, and a Women's Land Army, which recruited 1.5 million nonfarm women, eighteen and older, to work on farms. These focused efforts paid off: American food production during the war increased 32 percent over the Depression years 1935 to 1939.[60]

In 1942 the federal government instituted sugar rationing; later, rationing was extended to commercially prepared fruit, vegetables, meat, milk, eggs, and other foods. At the same time, dietitians came under pressure from CPS administrators to keep food costs down as the expand-

Americans line up to receive sugar rations in Detroit, 1942. (*National Archives, College Park, Maryland*)

ing program continued to tax the resources of supporting church constituencies. Civilian Public Service officials kept records of food expenditures in each of the camps, and dietitians tried to keep these statistics as low as possible. The average cost of feeding an assignee ranged from thirty-nine cents per day, when the United States first entered the war, to seventy-five cents per day, after food prices rose sharply.[61]

To keep costs in check, dietitians at CPS locations around the country experimented with subsistence projects. They planned large-scale gardens, acquired livestock, and enlisted campers with farm backgrounds to direct these ventures. Elizabeth Hernley, dietitian at a camp in Henry, Illinois, gardened with C.O.s on "a plot of nearly four acres which yielded 'over-abundantly.' "[62] Faced with bushels of green beans and other vegetables at harvesttime, she, like dietitians at other camps, taught courses in canning and preserving to interested assignees.

In addition, many CPS camps received food donations. For many mothers, wives, and sisters of conscientious objectors, preparing food for men in CPS became a significant expression of support for the program. Thousands of American women gardened with CPS in mind and then canned and dried large quantities of fruits, vegetables, and meats.[63] In

1943 MCC centralized the organization of canned and dried food contributions from American Mennonites. The agency established twenty-four collection centers across the country, providing cans and labels as well as transportation of food to Civilian Public Service camps. After the war ended and the camps were closed down, MCC converted the canning operation to a food-for-relief program.[64]

Far from the War Zone

Historian Robert Westbrook has noted that in wartime women tend to be geographically distant from battlefields and poorly informed about developments; as a result, women may be less skeptical than men about the official information they receive.[65] During World War II staff women for Civilian Public Service discovered that even while they lived and worked amid skeptics, physical distance from combat made it seem unreal. Mary Emma Showalter, a consulting dietitian who visited many CPS camps, recorded in her diary during a trip to California: "I sat out under the tall pines with the wind whistling through them. . . . Out here one would never know of the turmoil and strife taking place over the world."[66] Dietitian Nancy Foster, writing to her family from a camp in Ohio, expressed the same sentiment:

> On days like this it doesn't seem possible that there could be a war. My imagination isn't good enough to realize it very often, anyway. We have so much, and we're so safe, and reasonably happy, that I can't remember the suffering people in the rest of the world very often. I think about such things in the morning in meditation — and then come over here [to the kitchen] and get busy and focus on my own problems.[67]

The irony that so many conscientious objectors were to be sequestered in tranquil, sparsely populated settings for the duration was not lost on either the men or the women who served in CPS. Some would have preferred to do humanitarian work in a war zone, but U.S. policy prohibited Civilian Public Service assignees from leaving the country. After years of waiting, many of these C.O.s would contribute to postwar reconstruction efforts in Europe and elsewhere. But as long as the war continued, CPS staff members and assignees remained in their home front enclaves. Some were marking time until the war ended and they could resume normal lives.

Others immersed themselves mentally in the war by articulating cri-

Keeping up with news of the war in 1945 at the CPS library, Ypsilanti State Hospital, Ypsilanti, Michigan. (*Mennonite Library and Archives, Bethel College, North Newton, Kansas*)

tiques of it and envisioning alternatives to it. While these Americans did not enter CPS to pursue the contemplative life, aspects of camp experience invited it. Camp libraries, developed by the sponsoring church agencies as part of their educational goals for the alternative service program, were rich in philosophical, theological, and political discourse. Library collections included books, newspapers, and periodicals donated by supporters of CPS, as well as materials loaned by churches, colleges, and even local public libraries. "I am [reading] Vera Brittain's account of the bombing of Germany. . . . I wish everyone in the United States could read it; especially those who think we are pursuing a humane war," dietitian Nancy Foster wrote in 1944.[68] Discussions on the war, pacifism, politics, religion, and ethics dominated camp life; CPS women as well as men found themselves in polyglot communities where antiwar theorists introduced each other to Greek Orthodox, Jehovah's Witness, and Quaker perspectives.

Some sought out fellow C.O.s with similar interests and pursued common goals. At the AFSC camp at Trenton, North Dakota, for example, a "co-op group" met regularly to discuss the formation of a community that they hoped would model economic and social justice in the postwar world. Mary Wiser, one of the wives who joined in these gatherings, recalled that "it wasn't all rosy. The communal life of CPS became *very* wearing after three years, turning four of our close friends away from community [ideals] for life."[69] Some members of the small group began to look for ways to get out by seeking transfers to other CPS projects. But others made lifelong habit of the ideals they had nurtured in Civilian Public Service. In 1946 Mary Wiser and her husband, Arthur, joined the Macedonia Co-op Community in north Georgia, where they and other CPS alumni studied the causes of war and sought communal forms of work, recreation, and worship as alternatives. Several years later, they joined the Society of Brothers (now known as the Hutterian Brethren), where for nearly fifty years they have lived in community with other pacifists, including five couples they met in Civilian Public Service. "By uniting C.O.s from all over and from all ranks, CPS did us a great service," says Mary Wiser.[70]

Beginning in 1943 approximately twelve CPS locations offered specialized schools for C.O.s with particular interests. Selective Service permitted assignees to apply for transfers to units where they wanted to work or study. Among the best known of these magnet schools were the BSC-sponsored camp at Waldport, Oregon, attracting men skilled in the fine arts; the MCC-sponsored Farm and Community School near Hagerstown, Maryland, where C.O.s experimented with small-scale subsistence projects intended to demonstrate effective farm management to returning veterans; and an AFSC-sponsored unit in Gatlinburg, Tennessee, where conscientious objectors studied race relations.[71]

Staff women entered into the intellectual ferment of CPS with varying degrees of commitment, depending on their own interests and background.[72] Kitchens and infirmaries, where CPS staff women conducted much of their work, were venues for lively discussions. But women in CPS also had different concerns than did male staff members and assignees. Some of these concerns they articulated, while others remained largely unspoken.

It was difficult for any woman in CPS not to be sensitive to the inequities of conscription that thrust more than a million American soldiers into combat divisions but shielded conscientious objectors from harm. Married women who joined their husbands on the staffs of CPS camps reflected on their good fortune but recognized that they were no more deserving than other American women whose loved ones were sent to the front. Thus some CPS women also struggled with guilt. Immersing themselves in the demands of their jobs helped to assuage it; so did befriending lonely assignees whose wives or fiancées were far away.[73]

Like many men, some women in CPS also battled feelings of loneliness and depression. These emotions were acute among those who found themselves the sole woman among CPS assignees, or whose living quarters were primitive — literally, in one case, a "partitioned room in a tool shed."[74] A few nurses and dietitians struggled with unwelcome sexual attention from male acquaintances in the camps. Bessie Moyer, a nurse, felt "severe mental and emotional shock" when a married CPS assignee came into her cabin late one night and tried to kiss her; she threw him out and the next day was angered further by his refusal to apologize.[75] Not all women stayed in CPS for the duration; some left frustrated by conflicts with boorish camp directors. At a South Dakota camp, forty CPS men signed a petition supporting the camp nurse and dietitian who had clashed repeatedly with the camp director; nevertheless, the director retained his position while the nurse and several other women staffers resigned.[76] Sometimes the wives of camp administrators left fatigued by heavy workloads or because they wanted to devote more time to caring for young children. Other staff women left after seeing the demoralizing effect of CPS on conscientious objectors who found the program too confining.[77]

For most staff women, however, the positive aspects of Civilian Public Service work outweighed the negative. Like other World War II era women who were joiners, from Red Cross workers in China to "farmerettes" who signed on with the Women's Land Army, CPS staff women gained self-confidence. Even if their work went unnoticed by Americans intent on winning the war, they enjoyed the camaraderie of fellow pacifists, formed close friendships, managed crises, and derived a sense of achievement from working in settings where their skills were in demand.

Experiences in CPS encouraged personal and professional growth at a time when these women were young and, in many ways, impressionable. One dietitian recalled her extreme shyness as a college graduate beginning her first assignment at an all-male camp. Over a period of several years, she grew comfortable in a variety of camp settings, gaining confidence in public speaking and personnel management. Eventually, she confided to her diary the satisfaction of being at ease in a large roomful of men.[78] Another woman, whose Presbyterian family tolerated but did not identify with her husband's C.O. stance, spent two years as a CPS dietitian and cooking school instructor. A half century later she reflected that while her prewar university training as a home economist had not fully prepared her for it, CPS had been "the experience of a lifetime."[79]

From the time of their recruitment until the war ended, American women living among conscientious objectors as dietitians, nurses, and matrons explored their own peace convictions. After Civilian Public Service disbanded, many of these women moved into assignments abroad. Others, after putting ambitions on hold to follow their C.O. husbands, launched postwar careers as licensed dietitians, psychiatric nurses, or educators.[80] For these women, working with C.O.s—whose cause they shared—contributed to a sense of purpose and usefulness in time of war.

5 Collegiate Women Pacifists

During the Second World War a small minority of American college women explored ways to demonstrate their peace convictions to a skeptical, and sometimes hostile, public. Like drafted C.O.s, these women viewed alternative service work as a "moral equivalent of war." They devoted their energies to peace activism and to offering support and friendship to conscientious objectors, and their persistence led to the creation of all-women Civilian Public Service units.

Many of these women became part of networks at liberal arts colleges affiliated with the historic peace churches. While the federal government operated the Army Specialized Training Program and other military institutes on campuses across the country, peace activism remained strong at more than a dozen liberal arts colleges where administrators and professors recruited for Civilian Public Service.[1] These colleges produced many young career-minded women who embraced the C.O. position and supported the cause by moving to CPS sites to join conscientious objectors in their work.

Institutions in higher education with Quaker, Mennonite, and Brethren ties channeled thousands of students into the Civilian Public Service program. Administrators of the historic peace church colleges conferred with each other regularly about the impact of conscription on their schools. In August 1942 seven colleges, most with Mennonite constituencies, formed a coalition to promote campus alternatives to military training. These schools, all of which had students involved in Civilian Public Service, were Bethel, Hesston, and Tabor in Kansas, Freeman in

South Dakota, Goshen in Indiana, Bluffton in Ohio, and Messiah Bible in Pennsylvania.[2] The Church of the Brethren also sponsored colleges with significant numbers of students who joined CPS, including Juniata and Elizabethtown in Pennsylvania, Bridgewater in Virginia, Manchester in Indiana, McPherson in Kansas, and La Verne in California. Quaker-affiliated colleges, too, including Haverford, Swarthmore, and Bryn Mawr in Pennsylvania, Earlham in Indiana, Friends in Kansas, and George Fox in Oregon, were well represented among CPS assignees and volunteers.

With the exception of Haverford and Bryn Mawr, these sectarian schools were coeducational. But wartime circumstances precluded normal campus life. By 1943, as more and more men left, some coeducational institutions seemed almost like all-women colleges. A Mennonite student wrote to her friends in CPS: "When man planned wars, he certainly didn't take into consideration the separation of men and women. We girls are getting as tired of being with just girls as you are of being with just fellows."[3] Frances Clemens, who spent the war years as a student at Juniata College, described the mass exodus of young men from her campus. One day in March 1943 the entire student body walked to the train station of Huntingdon, Pennsylvania, to send off thirty students who had been drafted. The editors of the 1943 Juniata yearbook listed the names of these young men under the heading "Servicemen," making no distinction as to whether they had accepted active military duty or had obtained C.O. status and entered Civilian Public Service camps.[4]

Although the political and theological climates of these schools were conducive to pacifism, many students who remained on campus felt uncomfortable sitting on the sidelines while the nation waged war. Women students were generally relieved that their government demanded less of them than it did of men. Yet they were well aware that had they been male, they would have had to go before local draft boards to defend their stance.

The antidote to isolation was campus activism. The war had a profound impact on the lives of these college women, even though they studied and worked thousands of miles from the front lines. The women on these campuses blended idealism with pragmatism, taking courses in nutrition and nursing. Myrtle Molzen, a Bethel College alumna, wrote to Mennonite relief agency officials: "Please enter my name on the list of women who are eager to help demonstrate that . . . we are more than willing to give our service and even our lives to relieve human suffering. . . .

Surely the world has a right to expect absolute devotion to our cause from those of us who cannot shoulder the guns of the world, when thousands of young men are risking their lives."[5] At Bluffton College in Ohio, where the war depleted the class of 1945 to a cohort of thirteen, student life literally revolved around plans for postwar relief and reconstruction. Student peace organizations at schools like Bethel and Bluffton thrived while prominent antiwar organizations with memberships of mostly older women, like the Women's International League for Peace and Freedom, lost scores of members and held few public meetings.[6]

Pacifist Networks

College-age women who moved back and forth between school and the labor force or voluntary work assignments wanted to respond compassionately to human need and to share with male C.O.s the experience of alternative service. Although they were never drafted, young women took part in peace-oriented organizations at churches and colleges. Within these circles of acquaintanceship they enjoyed supportive relationships despite unorthodox political views.

In the years leading up to World War II thousands of women pacifists who had entered colleges or universities or begun careers in major cities had found soul mates in ecumenical peace organizations. In 1939 Margaret Calbeck, an alumna of the Ohio State University, moved to St. Paul to begin a position with the Young Women's Christian Association. Raised a Methodist, she had spent the previous summer with a student peace organization sponsored by the American Friends Service Committee. When she arrived in St. Paul, she was eager to establish connections with like-minded activists, so she contacted Twin Cities peace leaders whose names she had obtained from AFSC staff. In St. Paul she joined the Pacifist Action Fellowship (PAF), an organization affiliated nationally with both the Fellowship of Reconciliation and War Resisters League.

In dozens of American cities the Peace Action Fellowship functioned as an umbrella organization for small peace teams in local colleges and neighborhoods. Teams met weekly to discuss ways of promoting peace, to oppose legislative enactment of conscription, and to prepare for conscription in the likelihood of its passage. In the Twin Cities, PAF teams came together once a month to work on service projects, produce plays, listen to speakers, or simply to socialize. Fifty years later, Calbeck recalled the members of her fellowship as serious, single young people trying to find themselves in a threatening world. Almost none were members of historic peace churches; we were Methodist, Presbyterian, Episcopal, Lutheran, Reformed, Catholic, Jewish, and more. Many of these denominations had active Peace Fellowships at the national level (often affiliated with the Fellowship of Reconciliation), but at the local church level, a PAF member might well be the only pacifist in his home congregation or family.[7]

Thus, idealistic young people turned to Pacifist Action Fellowships for the kind of support that members of historic peace churches found in their congregations and families. In the Twin Cities PAF, Margaret Calbeck became acquainted with many men who would eventually choose Civilian Public Service over military service. She supported them by speaking at rallies against the Burke-Wadsworth conscription bill and, later, by organizing farewell parties for friends who had been drafted and were leaving for CPS camps around the country.[8]

In the fall of 1942 Calbeck returned to Columbus, Ohio, where she discovered that several of her Minnesota friends had been assigned to a CPS camp less than fifty miles away. She asked her parents if she might use their home to host a social for the C.O.s, and they agreed, even though her father was a veteran of World War I and her brothers were serving in the military. Calbeck was more fortunate than many other young women of her generation who adopted antiwar positions independently of family members; not all managed to integrate satisfactorily the two worlds in which they moved. With varying degrees of success, women like Margaret Calbeck struggled to find ways to express their convictions while bridging the gulf separating them from family members who supported the war.

Young pacifist women also struggled with the realization that few avenues of peace advocacy were open to them. In 1941 Alice Hostetler, a Mennonite, entered Northwestern University to earn a master's degree in organ performance. She joined the local chapter of the Fellowship of Reconciliation and a PAF team at the First Methodist Church in Evanston. By that time Congress had enacted conscription, and Peace Action Fellowships were shifting their focus to other issues, such as interracial work projects and research.[9] Hostetler enjoyed her contacts with student activists who were working for civil rights, but she yearned for a more visible and purposeful role in advocating peace.

While in Evanston, Hostetler corresponded with Mennonite friends serving in Civilian Public Service camps. Citing the pressures on civilians to buy victory bonds or to join "ten percent clubs," Hostetler wrote that Americans' patriotic fervor was incessant and tiresome. She told the men that women had few chances to demonstrate their convictions and declared that "we are looking to you fellows of CPS as 'candles in the night' to keep burning."[10] In a humorous aside, however, she told of her private resolve to undermine government propaganda. At the cafeteria where she worked pats of butter were molded with mottoes such as "Keep 'em Flying," "Remember Pearl Harbor," "Buy Defense Stamps." She added, impishly, "I've been serving them upside down all summer."[11]

Relief Training Schools

As civilians relatively unencumbered by family and financial responsibilities, collegiate pacifist women sought to serve on the home front in roles comparable to those available to WACs and WAVES in the armed forces. Ironically, the politics of gender offered pacifist coeds a choice that eluded male C.O.s: women could voluntarily enter service positions to demonstrate the depth of their convictions. A Goshen College graduate who became involved in mental health work during the war explained: "I was motivated to show the world that C.O.s were not slackers but were willing to serve in positive ways."[12]

From 1942 to mid-1943 these women hoped to join male conscientious objectors in preparing for CPS assignments overseas. The AFSC, MCC, and BSC were already involved in foreign relief work, and they wanted to establish special CPS schools to train workers to assist war victims. In late 1942, at the urging of Eleanor Roosevelt and others, Selective Service gave preliminary approval for the agencies to design a "CPS Training Corps" at four Mennonite, four Brethren, and four Friends colleges. During the spring and early summer of 1943 agency officials assigned 250 CPS men to three new locations: a "Foreign Relief and Rehabilitation Project" at Haverford College and relief workers' training schools at Goshen College and Manchester College.[13]

In June 1943, at the invitation of Chinese officials, a group of seven CPS men and one other volunteer left the Quakers' Philadelphia retreat center Pendle Hill to work under British direction in war-stricken areas of West China. Meanwhile, at Haverford, Goshen, and Manchester, the relief training schools began preparing additional contingents of C.O.s to work abroad. The AFSC, MCC, and BSC covered the schools' operating costs; college administrators and faculty set up curricula and directed the training programs.

Significantly, all three of the relief training schools were coeducational. This policy was a response to petitions from women who, like many men in Civilian Public Service, wanted to go abroad. Haverford College offered a special course for women in reconstruction work, and the AFSC also planned to open an all-women CPS unit at the Philadelphia State Hospital.[14] The organizers of the relief training schools at Goshen and North Manchester accepted women applicants who were college graduates or who school administrators had recommended as good candidates for nursing, social service, or clerical support positions in war zones.[15] In June 1943 sixteen women came to Goshen and four to Manchester to join CPS men in three-month courses in language study, history, public health, and social work. These women paid their own expenses. Most were unmarried, but some had husbands or fiancés who were also entering relief training. These couples hoped eventually to receive joint assignments for work abroad.[16]

The relief training schools were barely underway when C.O.s learned that they would not be permitted to go overseas. Veterans' organizations, angered by news reports of C.O.s en route to China as well as the opening of relief training schools, lobbied officials in Washington to prohibit conscientious objectors from going abroad. They protested that C.O.s were receiving college-level education at taxpayers' expense and argued that the national interest would be compromised if foreigners realized that the United States had "disloyal" citizens.[17] Peace church leaders regarded the campaign as evidence that veterans feared that war relief work would glamorize the public image of conscientious objectors.

The campaign touched a sensitive nerve in Washington, and in late June, Congress passed a rider to the Military Establishment Appropriations Act. Authored by Joseph Starnes of Alabama, the rider banned C.O.s from engaging in foreign relief. Though Selective Service had already approved overseas relief service assignments for conscientious objectors, the rider prohibited the use of army appropriations for such work. Even though the peace churches were prepared to finance CPS relief operations, their plans faded when congressional officials determined that General Hershey, the head of Selective Service, was not authorized to approve C.O.s' transfers outside the United States.[18]

The impact of the Starnes legislation was immediate: the Quaker-sponsored group en route to China turned back in midcourse, and the

Members of the China Unit, specializing in disaster relief training and based at Philadelphia, May 1943. Front row, from left: Howard Sollenberger, Wilson Head, Lea Spring. Back row: Ralph Rudd, Herbert Hadley, Robert Kreider, Rupert Stanley. Two other members are not pictured. (*American Friends Service Committee, Civilian Public Service, Swarthmore College Peace Collection, Swarthmore, Pennsylvania*)

Haverford, Goshen, and Manchester relief training schools disbanded. This was a serious setback to conscientious objectors who had hoped to contribute their services abroad. Since the late nineteenth century, the historic peace churches had been active in missions and humanitarian work in China, India, the Middle East, and Europe. During the First World War the AFSC had operated an ambulance unit in France. As historian Paul Toews suggests, religious objectors had long wished to demonstrate that their response to war was "constructive."[19] To their profound disappointment, organized opponents of conscientious objection would limit their opportunities to do so through the remainder of the war. In 1944, however, MCC did manage to send a few Canadian and American nurses to Great Britain. Ellen Harder, a Kansan who had been staffing a CPS camp infirmary in northern California, remembered: "When the call came to go overseas I couldn't say no because 150 men would have loved the opportunity."[20]

Although the Starnes Amendment prohibited colleges from hosting relief training units, after mid-1943, peace church leaders refocused their efforts and began preparing workers for *postwar* reconstruction. Civilian Public Service officials obtained permission from Selective Service to open new relief training units at state mental hospitals where conscientious objectors were working as aides. From 1943 through 1945, the AFSC, MCC, and BSC operated training units for CPS men and interested women at hospitals in Chicago; Denison, Iowa; Durham, North Carolina; Howard, Rhode Island; Poughkeepsie, New York; Ypsilanti, Michigan; Mulberry and Orlando, Florida; and Beltsville and Laurel, Maryland.[21] By 1945 approximately eight hundred conscientious objectors, a third of them women, had taken courses in the various relief training programs. They continued to hope that the Starnes rider would be repealed, but despite lobbying by peace groups, it remained intact in each year's military appropriations bill. Finally, after the war had ended, more than one thousand Friends, Mennonite, and Brethren CPS alumni were able to go to Europe, Asia, and elsewhere as volunteers for rehabilitation work.[22]

The "C.O. Girls"

Prior to 1943, Civilian Public Service openings were available only to women who wanted to work as dietitians, nurses, matrons, or secretaries. But social workers, teachers, and other women who had participated in the relief training schools began to press for more openings. In particular, college women who identified themselves as conscientious objectors sought to become part of CPS.

The agitation of women pacifists for meaningful work had roots in the interwar period. For example, during the summer of 1939, Edna Ramseyer, a doctoral student in home economics at the Ohio State University, had participated in a coeducational Quaker work camp. Ramseyer spent 1940 in France working with Spanish refugee children. There she and fellow AFSC volunteers discussed the roles that might be available to American women in the eventuality of male conscription. When Ramseyer returned from Europe, she joined the faculty at Bluffton College and in the summer of 1943 went to Goshen College to teach nutrition at Goshen's short-lived CPS relief training school. Ramseyer discussed with campus women how they might become more active in alternative service and suggested that they join conscientious objectors who had been assigned as aides at state mental hospitals. She pointed out that such institutions were in dire need of workers, male *and* female.[23]

Ramseyer's proposals caught the imagination of a group of campus women. On 12 August 1943, they gathered at the administration building of Goshen College, hoping to convince CPS officials that American women ought to have more occasions to witness for peace. These self-proclaimed "C.O. Girls" drafted a constitution for a women's conscientious objector society:

Section I. Name

This group shall be known as the COGS.

Section 2. Purpose

a. To give expression to and to develop convictions on peace and war.

b. To assume our responsibility in supporting the stand taken by the young men.

c. To relieve human need because that work is consistent with our stand as Christians.

d. To disseminate information about the constituency of the Mennonite Church as to the present conditions, needs, and work being done.

e. To help our brothers bear the reproach of Christ before the world.

f. To strengthen the witness of the Christian peace movement through closer unity.

g. To build character and ideals of everyday living now so as to build a stronger next generation.

h. To assist in building morals in this time of a long and tedious war.

Section III. Membership

All girls who have earnest Christian convictions on war and peace, of high school age or draft age (or over) shall be enrolled on request.[24]

Throughout August the Goshen women held sessions to secure a more substantial role in alternative service. At the same time, on the campus of Ypsilanti State Hospital in Ypsilanti, Michigan, where approximately fifteen wives, girlfriends, and sisters of conscientious objectors were joining a new, year-round CPS relief training unit, a related chapter of "C.O. Girls" formed. Conscientious objectors were reading daily press reports about the debate in Congress over the Austin-Wadsworth proposal to draft women. At Ypsilanti, Amanda Ediger, a nineteen-year-old student who was earning college tuition by working as a ward attendant, expressed her concerns in a letter to her parents: "You know if they are going to conscript women, they will surely be able to take me. The only thing that could keep me out would be working in a mental hospital. They aren't making any provisions for C.O.s, either."[25]

At Indiana's Manchester College, a group of women who had participated in relief training drafted a set of recommendations for women's inclusion in Civilian Public Service at the request of M. Robert Zigler, director of the Brethren Service Committee. The Manchester women urged Zigler to add a woman to the administrative staff of BSC to oversee women's participation in Civilian Public Service, and they listed professions ranging from architecture to psychotherapy as areas in which women could contribute to war relief. The Manchester women declared:

> There is tremendous latent power to be found in the beliefs and spiritual strength of pacifist women. This power can express itself through the intellects, the physical capabilities, and the hearts of women of the pacifist way. We feel very deeply that concurrently with any steps that are taken to train women in various fields or to give them opportunities for volunteer service there should be a recognition of the far-reaching service they can render. . . .

> We would urge that service opportunities for women, to the greatest extent possible, be developed to coincide in quality and variety with the numerous interests and responsibilities women find in modern daily living. . . . In this country or in foreign relief work, in special training units or in individual homes, every woman who believes in the philosophy of pacifism can . . . be of real service to the cause in which she believes.[26]

By mid-1943, then, all three of the church agencies responsible for CPS were considering the potential for women's involvement in the program. Civilian Public Service administrators were willing to hear women's suggestions. But the openness of church officials did not mean that COGs on college campuses aggressively called for equal access or rights to Civilian Public Service work. Using a language of restraint, they styled themselves as effective advocates for change within patriarchal church structures.

The Goshen COGs agreed privately that in their writings and public speeches on the ideals of Christian pacifism, they would guard against appearances of being "anti-patriotic," stressing instead that they were loyal U.S. citizens. They would discipline themselves to "remember the principles of non-resistance" in presenting their case. They would strive to be "considerate, tolerant, constructive, and respectful." They also aimed to avoid confrontation with church leaders on whom they depended for support. One COG memorandum suggested that members "have a good friendly talk with the minister, get his reaction, ask him to push the idea, if he agrees."[27]

In August 1943 the Goshen "C.O. Girls" and their mentor Edna Ramseyer met with MCC chairman Peter C. Hiebert. Hiebert supported the women's efforts to become directly involved in CPS, but he warned of a possible backlash from conservative Mennonites. He suggested that the women reconsider their organization's name, which "might be offensive to certain groups," and that they coordinate their activities with church-wide junior sewing circles.[28] The Goshen COGs decided to keep their name and organizational identity intact, but they also took Hiebert's counsel seriously. "Don't talk organization — present the idea," they decided among themselves. "Don't mention too much about COGs."[29]

Within a week, Ramseyer appeared before the MCC Executive Committee to advocate that the agency hire a female administrator to coordinate women's involvement in Civilian Public Service. She left the meeting with the men promising to "better organize and serve our Mennonite girls in relief training . . . [and] our women who are 'attached' to our various CPS units."[30] Ramseyer declined to accept an administrative position herself when MCC officials offered it to her, however. Ultimately, of the three main church agencies responsible for Civilian Public Service, only one, the AFSC, hired a female administrator to give leadership to women's participation. The MCC and BSC maintained male-dominated bureaucratic structures.[31]

In their discussions of women's participation in CPS, church officials responded readily to the argument that the presence of COGs in mental hospital units would boost the morale of CPS assignees. Here was a solution to a vexing problem. As short-term workers, the COGs would bring enthusiasm and renewed energy to men who were weary of being in Civilian Public Service. Thus church officials viewed the matter pragmatically while the COGs themselves articulated a more complicated position. Doris Miller, a Goshen student who went to Ypsilanti, noted, "I was challenged to become a part of mental health work because of my own deep convictions. My motivation: to support CPSers and to contribute to peace."[32]

Throughout the war a creative tension existed between the COGs, who wanted to address human need as conscientious objectors in their own right, and church leaders, who utilized them to raise the esprit de corps of male conscientious objectors. Decades later, Edna Ramseyer told an interviewer that in leading the "C.O. Girl" movement, she had always emphasized a motif of *service*, never "a new role for women."[33] Nevertheless, by encouraging young women to participate more directly in Civilian Public Service, she implicitly raised the issue of replacing conventional gender roles with more fluid ones. Ramseyer observed that young pacifist women were pushing out the boundaries of what their parents and teachers expected of them. In encouraging students to cultivate significant work experiences, the "C.O. Girl" movement was a force for change against the odds of self-determination for World War II era Americans who were both female and conscientious objectors to war.

Women's Service Units in Mental Hospitals

From 1943 to 1946 approximately three hundred young women left fifty college campuses to join male conscientious objectors at eight state-run psychiatric institutions.[34] These women were eager to work in short-term assignments where human need was great, but they chose CPS work for other reasons as well, including the desire for travel, adventure, and sometimes to escape boredom with work or school. The monetary rewards, though minimal, also appealed to nineteen- and twenty-year-old women who liked the idea of joining friends away from home, earning spending money, and saving for college. Civilian Public Service was more attractive than doing clerical or domestic work.[35]

Mental health was an obvious area in which these young women could serve since, throughout the war, labor shortages were severe at state mental hospitals. These institutions could not compete with the comparatively high wages and patriotic appeal of work in war-related industries. At the Philadelphia State Hospital, for example, 1,000 workers were on the payroll before the United States entered the war, but within a year, the number of employees had dropped to 200. In 1943 the ratio of attendants to mental patients was 1 to 212; the ratio of nurses to patients, 1 to 170. The situation was exacerbated by extreme overcrowding. Although the Philadelphia State Hospital had an official capacity of 3,500 patients, it actually housed more than 6,000.[36] In response to the crisis Selective Service approved placement of conscientious objectors as workers in state mental hospitals. From 1943 through 1946 about 3,000 Civilian Public Service men worked in forty-one psychiatric institutions across the country.

In June 1943 the American Friends Service Committee initiated an all-women CPS unit at the Philadelphia State Hospital. Charles Zeller, the hospital's administrator, told Quaker leaders that he had been impressed by the CPS men who had already begun working at the institution and that he was "willing to try women of the same belief."[37] The hospital arranged for them to fill temporary civil service positions, and the American Friends Service Committee administered the new program. In contrast to the male C.O.s, who received almost no monetary compensation, the women earned wages of sixty dollars a month in addition to room and board. Although most of the women were saving money for college or graduate study, they jointly contributed some of their earnings to war relief and to support needy dependents of conscientious objectors.[38]

At first, nine college-age women worked in three shifts as attendants on women's wards. Members of this first CPS women's unit — and others that opened later — performed tasks that ran the gamut of 1940s-style institutional care, from cleaning up wards of human excrement with a hose, to monitoring the use of straitjackets, to helping doctors administer electroshock treatment. Alice Calder, a Quaker college graduate who worked at the hospital for six months, recalled that she was both physically and mentally exhausted by the end of her stint: "It was hard work. One was always on the alert, working as I did primarily with senile and other deteriorated women. It was discouraging to see nothing in the way of therapy and rarely any caring."[39]

The women's service unit at the Philadelphia State Hospital soon expanded, drawing recruits mainly from Quaker-related colleges who were planning careers as nurses, teachers, social workers, psychologists, and occupational therapists. The women in the unit lived together and held weekly meetings to discuss their responsibilities on the wards. On average, they worked six eight-hour days. During leisure hours they socialized with CPS men who also lived and worked on the premises. Here and at a few other CPS locations, women and men replicated college life. From 1943 until the war ended, women in CPS took courses for academic credit in nursing, social work, church history, political science, and foreign languages. Pacifist college instructors came to the hospitals to teach these classes as part of a broad educational program for C.O.s who planned to do reconstruction work in Europe after the war. The group at the Philadelphia State Hospital also established a Mental Hygiene Program and produced a monthly periodical, *The Attendant*, which documented the work of regular staff attendants and C.O.s in state institutions and called for a restructuring of mental health care in the United States. When the war ended, these C.O.s broadened their efforts for mental health care reform, establishing the National Mental Health Foundation.[40]

Two years after the organization of the first "Women's CPS" unit in Philadelphia, the American Friends Service Committee established a similar unit at the New Jersey State Hospital in Trenton. Meanwhile, Brethren and Mennonite agencies operated their own service units for women. Although the agencies drew participants mainly from college campuses, other women enrolled as well, including recent high school graduates and those with advanced degrees. In 1944 the Brethren Service Committee developed a year-round women's service program at Elgin State Hospital in Elgin, Illinois, and from 1944 to 1946 the Mennonite Central Committee opened summer service units at its headquarters in Akron, Pennsylvania, at mental hospitals in Howard, Rhode Island; Ypsilanti, Michigan; Wernersville and Norristown, Pennsylvania; Cleveland, Ohio; and Poughkeepsie, New York; and in social work at Gulfport, Mississippi. Most of the "C.O. Girls" worked in mental hospitals, but a few at the administrative offices of Mennonite Central Committee worked as secretaries in CPS and relief work, and during the summer of 1946, those at the Gulfport unit led recreational activities for rural children in the Jim Crow South.

In 1945 members of the women's unit at the Poughkeepsie hospital invited their Hyde Park neighbor, Eleanor Roosevelt, for tea one afternoon to discuss postwar opportunities for American women. The C.O. women were impressed with their famous guest, although she had sometimes clashed with CPS officials. A year earlier, in the June 1944 issue of *Ladies' Home Journal* and in two of her syndicated newspaper columns, "My Day," Roosevelt had exasperated American pacifists by saying that "the conscientious objector is not performing any service for the country" and therefore was entitled to neither government pay nor family allotments. "It is hard for the innocent dependents who must suffer," she had written, "but that is part of the burden which a conscientious objector assumes when he lives up to his beliefs."[41] But Roosevelt, who had four sons in military service, used kinder words after her summer 1945 visit with CPS men and women at the Poughkeepsie hospital. To "My Day" readers she wrote that the C.O.s working there had improved

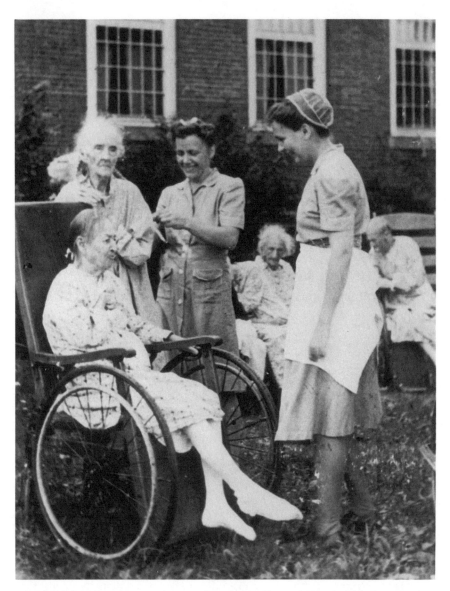

"C.O. Girls" with patients at the state hospital in Howard, Rhode Island, 1944. One of the Mennonite volunteers shown here wore a head covering as an expression of her religious identity. (*Mennonite Library and Archives, Bethel College, North Newton, Kansas*)

standards dramatically. Roosevelt's contacts with Mennonites and other C.O.s at Poughkeepsie led her to work closely with members of historic peace churches in the postwar years when she became a sponsor of the new National Mental Health Foundation.[42]

Some of the women who participated in the summer service programs

The Women's Summer Service Unit at Ypsilanti, Michigan, in 1945. These mental health workers served alongside male conscientious objectors on behalf of Mennonite Central Committee. (*Esther Rinner, Newton, Kansas*)

contributed in a tangible way to mental health reform. At the Cleveland State Hospital, CPS assignees and members of the women's unit filed reports citing abuse and neglect of patients. Their attempts at intervention went unheeded until brutal beatings by staff attendants led to the deaths of several patients. Documentation of these cases, provided in 1945 and 1946 to a grand jury by C.O. observers through the Philadelphia-based Mental Hygiene Program, gained national exposure with a lead story in a May 1946 issue of *Life*. The piece included a photo spread of patients in bleak ward settings with no access to occupational therapy or recreation. *Life*'s exposé led to reforms at the Ohio institution and focused national attention on the problems of state mental hospitals.[43]

The CPS women serving in state institutions came into constant contact with Americans who held C.O.s in disdain. Some of the college women reported that a "live and let live" attitude characterized their relationships with hospital staff.[44] But others faced daily hostility from hospital employees who had husbands, boyfriends, or sons in the military. These workers, offended by the presence of conscientious objectors, taunted them with names like "yellow coward," "yellow belly," or

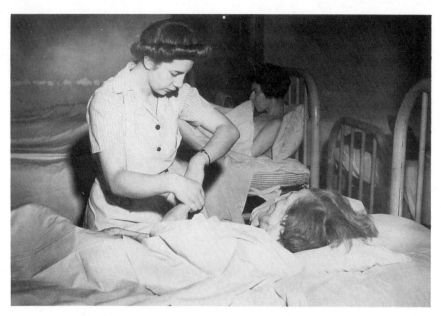

Ruth Miller volunteering at Cleveland State Hospital, 1946. (*Mennonite Historical Library, Goshen, Indiana*)

"canary." At Ypsilanti State Hospital a few employees put out an under-ground paper called *The Buttercup News*, which characterized the C.O.s in a derogatory way.[45]

One alumna of Friends CPS later reflected that the tensions that she and her C.O. coworkers had experienced in relationships with the regu-lar attendants had as much to do with class as with ideology: "They resented us for our pacifist views [and] because of our education and our wider options in seeking employment."[46] An alumna of Mennonite CPS recalled: "We COGs sometimes did extra things for the patients, such as giving a cold drink, and this made some of the other attendants a bit disgusted. We were 'spoiling' the patients."[47] Among some C.O.s and staff members, class-based tensions intensified. In February 1945 Mennonite Central Committee closed down a relief training unit at the Rhode Island State Hospital after regular staff members complained that conscientious objectors enjoyed shorter working hours and spent too much time in recreational activities.[48]

Despite the hostility that some of the CPS women encountered, they viewed their wartime experiences as unusually enriching. A member of the women's unit at the Philadelphia State Hospital reported at the end of her assignment: "Something happens that gives greater reality to our college education when we become part of the staff of a state hospital. . . . Through teaching patients to protect themselves from themselves, from others, and from their environment, we ourselves come to develop a fuller sense of self-reliance and inner security—precious qualities, indeed, for this changing world."[49]

When the war ended and Civilian Public Service began a two-year process of demobilizing conscientious objectors, the AFSC, MCC, and BSC expanded mental health service work through coeducational programs for college and noncollege youths. Thus what had been a cautious, experimental step in including women in alternative service became prologue to ambitious and multifaceted voluntary service programs for young people throughout North America.[50]

In 1943 advocates for women's participation in Civilian Public Service had argued that work in mental hospitals would strengthen women's peace convictions. In the short run, American conscientious objectors hoping to demonstrate their willingness to serve society in wartime found an opening in psychiatric institutional care, which was obviously in need of reform. In the long run, many C.O.s, men and women, found that the chance to work in a state hospital stimulated a lifelong interest in mental health. Civilian Public Service, which functioned as a wartime extension of higher education for thousands of conscientious objectors, had also contributed significantly to the welfare of the nation's most neglected citizens.

FREE
Conscientious
Objectors
U.S. *from* prisons

6 In the Aftermath of War

In 1944 three women students at Bethel College in Kansas wrote new lyrics to the tune of the well-known World War II song "Bell Bottom Trousers." They recorded their version and sent a tape to a friend in Civilian Public Service who was engaged to one of the women. The "blue denim" of the refrain was a reference to the poverty of conscientious objectors:

Once there was a girl who worked her way through school,
She loved a Conchie, and he loved her too.
When he went to CPS at only twenty-three
She wished that she were sitting on his knee.

> Blue denim trousers, coat of denim, too
> She loved a Conchie, and he loved her too.

When the war is over, he'll be coming back
And then it's only money that they'll lack.
Soon they will settle down and raise a family
They'll live together, ever happily.[1]

This satire, conveyed as a private message between friends and lovers, underscores the conventionality of the dreams harbored by many of the young adults associated with Civilian Public Service.[2] Popular literature appearing in the mid-1940s supported the notion that American women looked forward to a blissful future at home, devoting themselves to child rearing rather than remaining in the labor force. But the Kansas students who penned these verses were not just reflecting the social conservatism that seemed to be the order of the day. They were also mocking it, for more than a thousand Americans who had been part

Robert and Rachel Fisher, C.O. couple in private quarters at Ypsilanti State Hospital in Michigan, near the end of the war. (*Mennonite Library and Archives, Bethel College, North Newton, Kansas*)

of CPS, including many women, would defer domestic impulses after the war. As the demobilization of American troops and CPS assignees became imminent, conscientious objectors who had been eyeing humanitarian work abroad knew that they would finally be able to travel to Europe, Asia, and the Middle East for postwar rehabilitation assignments.[3]

After the mid-August announcement of Japan's surrender, Americans across the country celebrated the end of the war, and in many quarters, conscientious objectors joined in. On V-J Day, three couples associated with the CPS camp at Denison, Iowa, took their five children and "pooled our money to buy one large can of baked beans and one watermelon, and went out to a roadside park to celebrate."[4] But the bombing of Hiroshima and Nagasaki tempered American jubilation. A Mennonite woman recalled that she and her husband had joined a carload of C.O. friends from New Jersey to revel in the streets of Philadelphia, but afterward the group had returned to their CPS unit somber and depressed about the effects of the atomic bombing.[5] A Quaker woman expressed her anxiety in an August 1945 letter to her C.O. husband, who had recently begun a five-year prison term for violating the Selective Training and Service Act. While awaiting the birth of their first child, she wrote:

Margarita Will, social worker and CPS wife, visiting a rural family near Castañer, Puerto Rico, 1945. (*Margarita Will, Seattle, Washington*)

"Still no signs of Junior's debut. I think he's waiting till the war's over and people stop officially murdering each other. I hope that news comes any minute now, although I shan't celebrate 'victory' — it's been too horribly costly. I don't know what it will mean to the two of us personally and the others in our positions — that depends, I guess, on how vindictive our government is."[6]

Costs of Nonconformity

Vindictive or not, federal policies governing the demobilization of World War II objectors were conspicuously less generous than provisions for military personnel. Men in CPS were denied the benefits guaranteed to veterans by the Servicemen's Readjustment Act of 1944. This "GI Bill of Rights" designated federal funds for veterans' education and vocational training, including tuition, fees, and living allowances, as well as health coverage, unemployment insurance, and loans for building homes or starting new businesses. During the spring of 1944 a CPS staff woman, aware that C.O.s could expect no such government assistance, paused from her routine to reflect:

> Sometimes when I look at all these men — and boys — I wonder what will become of them. I would hazard, roughly, that a third were interrupted before they'd finished school, of which the vast majority probably won't go back. A scant third have something to go back to — a farm, a family store, a job that's being held for them for the duration — there are precious few in that last category, though. And there are a few who'll land on their feet regardless. . . .

> [But] what of the chemists who've been away from chemistry three years already? And the boys who knew they were going to be drafted and never bothered to get anything but fill-in jobs? It's no wonder that CPS men think of farms and farming seriously. At least that way they'll eat.[7]

Many C.O.s were concerned that they would have trouble finding jobs in a market crowded with veterans, and some wondered how their applications would be received at colleges and graduate schools. Few had been able to save money during the war. During the long process of CPS demobilization, from October 1945 through March 1947, C.O.s tried to overcome these obstacles. Many drew on the financial resources of their families to resume or pursue new interests in schooling and work.[8] Others, particularly those in urban areas, received help from "local demobilization committees" composed of persons belonging to a coalition of peace organizations. By the fall of 1945, welcoming committees in eighteen major U.S. cities from New York to Los Angeles were positioned to help conscientious objectors find suitable housing and employment.[9]

Church groups and individuals responded generously to appeals from the historic peace church agencies to assist men released from Civilian Public Service. Sewing and mission societies that had long provided food, clothing, and other essentials were more than willing to provide funds for the postwar education of conscientious objectors. After all, as one Mennonite woman reminded her friends, "churches of other denominations voted large sums to memorialize the boys from their congregations who served in the armed forces."[10] And professional women who for years had supported conscientious objectors continued to help them after their release, often by loaning them money.[11] Although American C.O.s received none of the generous governmental benefits available to veterans, they did have access to some resources in adjusting to postwar life. The support that most received from their families, friends, and churches helped immeasurably in counteracting the antagonism that awaited them in the postwar world.

Demobilizing Conscientious Objectors

On 25 May 1945, shortly after the U.S. army announced plans to partially demobilize American troops, Selective Service officials disclosed their proposal for demobilizing men in Civilian Public Service.[12] While the administration expected to release C.O.s so slowly that they would not arrive back in their communities earlier than American servicemen, Selective Service officials faced strong criticism. Local draft boards and veterans' groups, many of them dissatisfied with the pace of demobilization, charged that the agency was treating conscientious objectors permissively and lobbied Congress to reject the plan.[13]

Throughout the summer Selective Service officials wrangled with members of the House Military Affairs Committee over provisions for C.O. demobilization. Meanwhile, men in CPS who had been looking forward to imminent release began to worry, along with their families, that they would be forced to stay in government service for another year or two.[14] In August 1945 a CPS man complained in a letter to his parents that the climate of congressional debate was one of outright animosity. Men working in Civilian Public Service, he said, took offense when they heard statements like "Don't coddle the Conchies!"[15]

After V-J Day, Congress and the Truman administration came under increasing public pressure to bring American troops home. The federal government responded with remarkably prompt military demobilization. By December 1945 the War Department had granted release to approximately 60 percent of all service personnel who had been in the military at the end of the war. In the same period, however, Selective Service released only 10 percent of the men in Civilian Public Service.[16] This inequity in the federal government's treatment of C.O.s particularly incensed those who resented the conscription of their labor and who opposed working without compensation at jobs that were normally salaried. In May 1946 the *Washington Daily News* reported on the grievances of a

In 1946, conscientious objectors assigned to the CPS unit at College Park, Maryland, campaigned near the U.S. State Department for amnesty for imprisoned C.O.s. Left to right: Wesley De Coursey, his spouse, Verda De Coursey, and Lowell Yohe. (*Verda De Coursey, McPherson, Kansas*)

group of CPS assignees in Maryland, explaining: "They feel that now — with the war over and men looking for jobs — they are 'scab' labor."[17]

In June 1946 President Harry Truman signed legislation that extended for nine months the Selective Training and Service Act of 1940. Demobilization of both the armed forces and Civilian Public Service would proceed well into 1947. As the rate of CPS releases continued to lag behind military releases, frustration rose among the thousands of men still assigned to Civilian Public Service. Many questioned what they viewed as the sponsoring church agencies' complicity in peacetime conscription.[18] At some CPS camps assignees staged hunger strikes, work strikes, and slowdowns to protest the continuing policy of conscription and the government's discriminatory treatment of C.O.s. Especially in the camps at Glendora and Minersville, California; Gatlinburg, Tennessee; and Big Flats, New York, frustrated assignees demanded prompt release. A few left their posts without authorization. Those who participated in the "walkout" protests were among the last of the approximately six thousand World War II C.O.s who served time in prison.[19]

A Gallup poll conducted in December 1946 showed that 69 percent of Americans favored releasing C.O.s still in custody. For the nine months following March 1947, when the Selective Training and Service Act expired and the last CPS camps in Colorado, Virginia, and Maryland closed down, a host of peace associations, churches, and civil liberties organizations demanded amnesty for the three hundred American C.O.s still incarcerated. Prominent Americans including Pearl S. Buck, Harold L. Ickes, Reinhold Niebuhr, and Walter Reuther joined the campaign to restore rights to C.O.s in prison and on parole. Finally, on Christmas Eve 1947, President Truman signed a proclamation of "selective amnesty," pardoning most objectors who had violated the law for religious reasons but withholding pardon from those classified as political objectors.[20]

Telling the Story of Civilian Public Service

At the end of World War II, pacifist leaders across the country were taking part in discussions that ranged well beyond the scope of demobilization's impact on conscientious objectors. Delegates to the newly created United Nations were making the case for a strong military establishment and for the maintenance of peace through collective security. Congress began considering legislation that would institute a peacetime draft and universal military training.[21] These proposals met with opposition from many scientists, educators, labor organizations, and civil rights leaders, as well as pacifists. Throughout the war American peace groups had honed lobbying skills asserting the rights of conscientious objectors, resisting the conscription of women, and advocating the release of interned Japanese American citizens. In the months and years after the bombing of Hiroshima and Nagasaki, pacifist leaders hoped to put these skills to use in addressing the problems of refugees and displaced persons, challenging postwar conscription, and questioning the morality of atomic weapons.[22]

But few of the women who had participated in Civilian Public Service as staff, family members, volunteers, or benefactors entered into these discussions. Although several thousand women had had casual connections to the alternative service program through their husbands or friends, and hundreds of women had had stronger ties as CPS staff members and volunteers, during the years to come most of these women would say little publicly about their experiences as C.O.s on the American home front.

Four factors help to account for the paucity of women's perspectives on alternative service. First, in the immediate postwar period, Americans were absorbed in the task of reintegrating veterans—98 percent of whom were male—into civilian life. Enactment of the GI Bill helped to ensure the dominant place of veterans in American society. During the coming decades this World War II generation, known for its war stories and wounds, assumed the most visible positions of leadership in civic life and dominated cultural interpretations of the nation's wartime achievements. The experiences of other Americans, including conscientious objectors, received scant public notice.

Second, the historic peace churches responsible for the program rarely acknowledged the contributions of women. Throughout the war and during the period of demobilization, church agencies had solicited the support of women and had depended on them to sustain Civilian Public Service. Yet as it came to an end, the agencies gave little thought to the presence of women. One CPS alumnus who had served in a mental health unit at Howard, Rhode Island, said of his experience: "We owe much to our wives who have gladly served by our sides and have taken the same scoffing. . . . Their names shall go down in the annals of CPS."[23] He was overly optimistic about the level of recognition that C.O. women would receive, for in 1945, as administrators at the AFSC, BSC, MCC, and NSBRO arranged for the preservation of Civilian Public Service records, they tended to slight female participation. Research coordinators for the Mennonite Central Committee solicited from ex-CPS men (but not from women) autobiographical materials, comments, and criticisms regarding their alternative service experiences.[24] And the *Directory of Civilian Public Service,* an alumni handbook published in 1947 by the National Service Board for Religious Objectors, omitted the names of the hundreds of women who had lived and worked in CPS camps and units as dietitians, nurses, and matrons.[25]

Third, during the remainder of the 1940s and through the 1950s, many of the women who had been associated with Civilian Public Service stayed home to raise children. Others moved back and forth between domestic responsibilities and part-time or temporary positions in the labor force. Unlike male conscientious objectors, these women encountered few questions about their wartime work.

Finally, some women came to view World War II as both the cause and symbol of painful memories. During the war they had endured community hostility, strained or broken family relationships, economic burdens, and even job or housing discrimination. Like the men who had participated in alternative service, C.O. women faced an uncertain future. Some feared continued antagonism from acquaintances and co-workers. A few struggled to save troubled marriages. Some left college or graduate school prematurely due to financial pressures. Others faced lean years as veterans returned home and received preferential treatment in hiring over women *and* conscientious objectors.[26]

As a result, many of these women did not often speak of their past. "Those were years I have wanted to forget," acknowledged one wife who worked as a nurse in several CPS camps and whose children were born in 1942 and 1944. "To me it was deeply unnatural [to have camps] of all men, against their will, much as it must have been in the army. I longed for it to end. But possibly my life would have seemed less important and urgent had I not experienced those dark ages."[27]

Subsequently, when the subject of the war came up, many women who had taken part in Civilian Public Service found little common ground with Americans who had supported the war. To be sure, in wartime they had shared some of the feelings common to military families, such as loneliness and a sense of unease about the future. But in the decades to come, they knew that neither orthodox interpretations of the war nor popular images of American home front culture adequately took stock of *their* perspectives. Over time, some wondered why no one seemed interested in how they had spent the war years. Their sense of isolation was hardly unique. Decades after the war, other American women of the same generation, including former WACs, WAVES, aircraft workers, and shipyard workers lamented that their historic contributions during World War II seemed virtually forgotten.[28]

During the 1960s and early 1970s some women would privately recall their stories as they watched their children protest American involvement in the Vietnam War. But not until much later would they share publicly their World War II experiences. In the 1990s seven of the women contacted for this study indicated that they had written memoirs or were contemplating doing so.[29] One, a former CPS dietitian, told scholars at a conference commemorating the fiftieth anniversary of World War II that autobiographical writing "was a release for me. I had never been asked about my experience."[30]

Postwar Lives

Men and women who identified themselves as C.O.s often wondered how the stance they had taken would affect their lives in the postwar world. James Rutschman, a Kansan, spent more than four years in Civilian Public Service in North Carolina, Iowa, and Nebraska. When he and his wife Charlotte returned to their home community a year and a half after the war ended, they planned to take over the operation of Charlotte's family farm. But some neighbors, still bitter that in 1941 James Rutschman had appealed a local draft board decision and won a C.O. classification, sent letters warning that the Rutschmans were not welcome. (During CPS furloughs, when the couple had come back to the community for weeklong visits, they had kept low profiles at their parents' rural homes, too fearful to appear in town.) Disappointed but unwilling to face continued harassment, they moved away and gave up farming.[31]

Even decades after the war ended, some C.O.s were denied employment openings or professional benefits. One woman, an architect in partnership with her husband in Denton, Texas, related an incident from the 1970s:

> We applied for a job remodeling our county courthouse. Tom and others here had been counseling boys about their options if drafted for the Vietnam War and had sent Friends Peace Committee brochures to all high school seniors letting them know there was an alternative to military service.

> A reactionary paper's editor was aware of this and was a buddy of a commissioner. After they had verbally given us the job, he persuaded them to renege. Few people knew the inside story, though many friends knew Tom had been a C.O. By then we had a large body of Democratic, church, League of Women Voters, and college faculty friends who showed up en masse at the next county commission meeting to protest. It did no good.[32]

From Baltimore, another wife of a World War II C.O. explained how a recently enacted policy continues to discriminate against conscientious objectors. Her husband, drafted in 1941, spent four and a half years in Civilian Public Service in forestry and mental health work. After the war ended, he resumed his career as a public school teacher:

> When my husband retired, a bill was passed in the state of Maryland to give soldiers, navy, air force, marines, and even merchant marines,

who were not drafted, added retirement years. [For each ten months of government service, they earned credit for one year of teaching.] The legislature did not recognize C.O.s.

A representative of the Teachers' Association from Baltimore County tried to get the same status for Clarence, the only C.O. retiring, but it was not recognized. That would have made five years of teaching which would have increased his retirement [benefits]! So you see, even today we are experiencing a stand we took some fifty years ago.[33]

Her story serves as a bitter reminder of the inequities that C.O. couples faced during the war as a result of federal policies. Some families of conscientious objectors also experienced crises during the Communist scare of the late 1940s and early 1950s when a number of states adopted loyalty oaths. Across the country, conscientious objectors who refused on principle to take the oath lost their jobs. In recent years some World War II C.O.s have used the Freedom of Information Act to gather evidence of the FBI's scrutinizing of their personal lives when they were in their twenties or thirties.[34] Yet despite evidence of some continued discrimination against American C.O.s, these persons remain committed to the tenets that they embraced during World War II.

Legacies of Civilian Public Service

A pacifist subculture in America persists more than fifty years after World War II. One remarkable network of women attests to the ethos of community that has long infused it: each year, a round-robin letter still circulates among a group of twenty-seven CPS wives. These women, mostly Amish and Mennonite, have kept in touch since 1946, when the CPS camp at Terry, Montana, closed down. During the war years these women rented rooms or shared housing near an old CCC camp where their husbands and friends were assigned to work on a government irrigation project. After the war, one of the wives made a list of all the CPS-related women who had lived in Terry. She wrote a letter, tucked it into an envelope with an address list, and mailed it to the woman whose name appeared next on the list. Even now, the survivors of this circle look forward each year to receiving a packet crammed with letters from their CPS friends.[35]

Elizabeth Goering, one of writers of the round-robin, reflects on how it serves both as a gauge of pacifist conviction and a mechanism for documenting women's lives:

As careers became established and families took less time and energy, some [letter writers] told of becoming more and more their own persons, of greater involvement in a broader spectrum of concerns. For some that meant remaining a part of the 'cutting edge' of that theology which had brought them together in the first place — the gospel of peace. For a few, it included becoming involved at the political level.

While some women went on to break with tradition, others continue to live quietly within their own communities. Now one can read about the annual ritual of spring housecleaning, of quiltmaking and quilting bees, reports from world travelers, of marches protesting militarism in our country, of involvement with Seniors for Peace, or about the work of a State Task Force on Aging.[36]

Like these women, thousands of CPS alumni have maintained contact with friends they learned to know through the program. Nearly all the women who contributed information for this study expressed appreciation for the bonds of friendship that evolved out of camaraderie with other conscientious objectors. Many of Civilian Public Service's 151 camps and units are commemorated with reunions held every two years or at less frequent intervals. These reunions confirm participants' continued commitment to conscientious objection.

Adaline Pendleton Satterthwaite, a physician living in Pennsylvania, reports that her ties with CPS friends have been close over the years, sustained by reunions and correspondence. In the spring of 1944, while working at Presbyterian Hospital in San Juan, Puerto Rico, she met Bill Satterthwaite, a conscientious objector assigned to CPS work on the island of St. Thomas. The couple married eight months later in San Juan in the presence of C.O. friends. Widowed in 1949 while living in China, Adaline Satterthwaite raised the couple's son and pursued a career in international medicine that took her back to Puerto Rico and then to Thailand, Pakistan, Venezuela, Peru, Nepal, and Bangladesh. Now retired, Satterthwaite contends that in World War II "it was possible to maintain one's pacifism and serve effectively."[37] Rose Weirich Yutzy, who followed her husband to an Illinois base camp in 1942 and later joined him in mental health work at a CPS site in New Jersey, explains why she still attends reunions as often as possible, even though her husband died twenty-five years ago: "I do feel definitely that *I* was in CPS."[38]

Despite their expressions of gratitude for the program, some women alumni recall agonizing over the philosophical implications of their choices. Americans who thought of themselves as conscientious objectors recognized that it was almost impossible for any citizen to avoid participating in the war effort. All who paid taxes certainly had a part in it, and conscientious objectors who performed government-sponsored civilian work sometimes worried that they were doing little more than taking the place of men who fought in the war. One respondent admitted that "we, my husband and I, look back and wonder if more CPS men had refused to register for the draft and gone to jail, if this might not have made a more profound statement."[39] Two women whose husbands were among the small minority of assignees who "walked out" of CPS asserted that they had fully supported the men's acts of protest.[40] Another respondent commented that in writing about alternative service, "it is hard for me to say 'I' instead of 'we' because we were so much together on the thinking and the decisions."[41]

In assessing the choices that they had made fifty years earlier, respondents offered highly personal perspectives. One mused that conscientious objectors might have tried harder to bridge the ideological gulf separating them from coworkers and neighbors: "We may have been overly concerned about our 'right' not to support the war, and unsympathetic with the plight of those who participated. Some of us were too fearful of censure."[42] Others, too, recognized that in debates over ideology, tolerance for other perspectives was easily shunted aside.

Some women admitted to having second thoughts about the war's validity. "At the time," said one, "I felt we were all victims of propaganda. Realizing the extent of Hitler's program later, I still haven't come to terms with [the war]."[43] A Church of the Brethren woman whose husband had been in Civilian Public Service for four and a half years reflected that during the war she had "not known where to turn for unadulterated information." Like many American pacifists, she had dismissed reports of Jewish persecution as propaganda, and to belatedly learn details of the Holocaust was highly distressing. Fifty years after the war, she still found it troubling that so few Americans had known what was happening to Jews in Germany and Poland. She added: "My Jewish friends made such remarks, but I could hardly believe this possible."[44]

Respondents offered candid appraisals of Civilian Public Service. A number of women remarked that because the program had been hastily organized and lacked precedent, it often fell short of expectations. Yet they also acknowledged that World War II C.O.s had enjoyed far more freedom of expression than had their predecessors in World War I. Almost unanimously, respondents credited Civilian Public Service with giving conscientious objectors opportunities for useful, humanitarian-oriented work. Many echoed the sentiment of Verda Lambright Kauffman, a Mennonite, that "democracy demands some compromise. CPS wasn't perfect, but it was worthwhile."[45]

Many women appreciated the financial autonomy, limited though it was, that they encountered in Civilian Public Service. Unlike their husbands, C.O. wives generally earned at least modest sums during the war. The wartime experience of drawing a paycheck and assuming economic responsibility helped to shape expectations for marital equality. And some women found that the communal orientation of CPS had a profound impact on their attitudes toward money and material possessions. Mary Elizabeth Handrich, a Michigan woman who earned her way as a maid while following her husband to CPS assignments in Pennsylvania, Montana, and Florida, remembered that immediately after the war her dreams of building and owning a house were deferred. Yet she was philosophical. "CPS helped me to realize that people are more important than things," she said. "Living simply frees a person."[46]

For many women, alternative service was a more intellectually stimulating environment than any they had known. Elizabeth Shetler Barge, a Mennonite, later recalled: "In CPS we were involved in discussions and activities that stretched our minds."[47] Civilian Public Service influenced women's educational and vocational plans. Some entered college immediately after the war to prepare for careers in health, education, or church work. But for others, the route to higher education was more circuitous. One CPS wife, who completed a bachelor's degree thirty-seven years after the war had interrupted her college studies, credited her achievement to the encouragement she had received from C.O. friends in the mid-1940s.[48] Another woman recalled that her association with musicians, poets, artists, theater professionals, and craftsmen at the fine arts CPS camp near Waldport, Oregon, "was exhilarating — the greatest experience of my life, and they are still our friends scattered all over."[49]

Women in Civilian Public Service prized the free exchange of ideas they encountered. One C.O. wife noted that CPS had stimulated her interest in gender issues: "[I] met other women . . . who were already years ahead of me in the women's movement, and I listened to them."[50] Others saw openings for change in the church. Lois Schertz, a Mennonite, recalled that as a member of a cohesive CPS unit, she discovered her aptitude for leading worship. Ruefully, she added: "I went back home after the war and it took a good thirty years for [women to be accepted in positions of church leadership]."[51]

Nearly all respondents indicated that their experiences had deepened their interest in peace concerns. Some went abroad soon after the war to participate in relief efforts and returned to the United States with an abiding interest in humanitarian work. Others who had not been affiliated with the historic peace churches eventually became Quaker, Mennonite, or Brethren as a result of their CPS associations. Over the years, many CPS alumni continued to support the work of the American Friends Service Committee, Mennonite Central Committee, and Brethren Service Committee. Since World War II these organizations have retained their emphases on peace and humanitarian service but have expanded their scope. Today their programs range from disaster relief, mental health services, and care for AIDS patients to victim/offender restitution programs and international visitor exchanges.

Women in CPS who spent the postwar years nurturing children sought to transmit to their sons and daughters values of peace, benevolence, and service. Sixty-eight of the women contacted for this study commented on their children's attitudes toward peace issues, all but one reporting that they had tried to raise their children to avoid or refuse participation in war. Sixty-five of these women said that their children are generally in agreement with their views. Some of the women pointed out that their daughters—who have never had to face conscription— have been strongly influenced by their pacifist upbringing. Only three women reported that one or more of their children had entered military service. Twenty-three reported that during the wars in Korea and Vietnam, their draft-age sons had declared themselves conscientious objectors. Most of these young men participated in alternative service; others went to prison or to Canada.[52]

In the 1960s and 1970s, those whose sons faced the draft during the Vietnam War found themselves reliving the nonconformist stance they had taken years earlier. While their children's decisions prompted them to draw parallels with their own experiences, they also recognized that the provisions for alternative service during the Vietnam War, which allowed C.O.s to design their own assignments, differed substantially from the camp-based program of CPS. Several respondents commented that they thought their children's experiences in protesting the Vietnam War had been more painful than their own experiences as World War II objectors. A former Civilian Public Service nurse explained: "My sons who resisted the Vietnam War did not have a network of friends going through similar experiences. In fact, they relate very well to our CPS friends."[53]

During the early 1960s, when President John F. Kennedy inaugurated the Peace Corps, he revived memories of Civilian Public Service and conscientious objectors' postwar voluntary service abroad. Some women who took part in CPS suggest that even today, Civilian Public Service can serve as a model against which to test national service programs for college-bound Americans. They cite AmeriCorps, which since 1993 has placed students in programs that focus on the environment, public safety, and human services, as a present-day program with linkages to World War II alternative service.[54]

In recent years, women alumni of Civilian Public Service have directed their considerable energies to a variety of pacifist organizations, among them Beyond War, Seniors for Peace, and the Women's International League for Peace and Freedom. They cite an array of interests: race relations, environmentalism, antinuclear activism, war-tax resistance, use of mediation techniques for resolving local conflicts, ministries for offenders, concern for the homeless, and women's health issues. These women report that they see themselves as living by principles that they espoused fifty years ago. From Ohio, one wrote that "it is important to move on to the present and future and not rest on what was done in World War II but to live so that others can respect our beliefs and be influenced by them."[55] Her comment underscores a conviction shared by many of these women — that now, in their retirement years, social activism remains a significant avenue for engaging the broader culture.

A half century ago, these women were marginal figures on the American home front. Many of them, raised in religious traditions that prized nonresistance and discouraged political participation, identified themselves as conscientious objectors to war but would have been reluctant to describe themselves as activists. Yet they found that their experiences with Civilian Public Service led to a broadening of perspectives that remained with them long after the war ended. As was true for millions of other Americans, the war offered them the chance to leave provincial communities. Pearl Mierau Janzen recalled that in 1943 she had barely turned nineteen when she left her Nebraska home to marry a man assigned to Civilian Public Service in South Dakota. Before the war ended, she had followed her husband to Michigan, given birth to a daughter, worked a succession of jobs to support herself and her child, and accepted an assignment as CPS dietitian in Idaho. Those days, she reflected, "forced me to think! I had to . . . walk against the stream of society."[56]

The women who associated themselves with Civilian Public Service did not all have similar experiences; it mattered a great deal whether they were financially comfortable or poor, single or married, working for wages or caring for children. But in spite of the diversity of their circumstances, they were motivated by a sense of responsibility to take a stand against the war. Although these women constituted a small fraction of America's home front citizenry, they charted a course that required complex ethical choices.

The American peace activist Dorothy Detzer, writing in 1948, observed that while wartime is difficult for any pacifist, it also provides compensations, including an occasion to measure the firmness of one's convictions and to discern who are one's friends.[57] Detzer's insights help to explain why so many women who objected to the Second World War now appraise their experiences positively, even though they recall being on the receiving end of personal insults and discriminatory policies. The multiple dimensions of their experiences—from testing their ideals against a militaristic national culture to discovering who they could count on for support—were lessons learned and kept.

Conclusion

During the 1940s American mobilization for war was a conservative operation in virtually every aspect, including the persistence of sex segregation both in the military sector and on the home front. Civilian Public Service, created by the federal government and administered by historic peace churches, reflected the conventional gender ideology of the era. Federally sanctioned provisions for conscientious objectors were directed solely toward men. As the alternative service program evolved, CPS administrators assumed that women would contribute in their habitual role as providers of moral and emotional support. In short, the architects of alternative service never envisioned that so many women would ultimately contribute to the program in so many ways.

Yet despite the limitations of this wartime institution, pacifist women stepped out of the gendered confines of tradition and worked in partnership with men. More than twelve thousand men were taking part in a national experiment in which they worked at government-assigned jobs without pay. The gradual and sustained involvement of several thousand pacifist women in this alternative service program — none of them subject to the draft — demonstrates the strong pull of nonconformity for *both* women and men whose family traditions emphasized religious community involvement over political and military participation.

In making choices that went against the broader culture, these pacifists held onto a long-cherished principle of avoiding participation in war. But the roots provided by religious subcultures, so stable in peacetime, were tested in wartime. Increasingly, American conscientious objectors became engaged in secular institutions, drawn by government-sponsored programs like Civilian Public Service that provided opportunities in health care, education, and social service. They hoped to demonstrate that while they were good citizens, they were not, in the phrase of Jean Bethke Elshtain, "wartime civic cheerleaders."[1]

Their deliberate and visible rejection of wartime mobilization reflected inherited traditions of religious pacifism more than concerns about gender equality. Unlike Jane Addams and other American pacifists who in the First World War had staked their claims for women's unique role as peacemakers, and unlike many women of the Vietnam War years who would link peace activism and feminism, the American women who took part in Civilian Public Service made no such assertions. Their actions were infused with ideals of humanitarian service that heralded principles of religious freedom but deemphasized gender. This poses an intriguing contrast to both the commitments of World War I era suffragists who demonstrated against the war and feminists of the Vietnam War era, and it suggests that scholars have yet more work to do in untangling the role of women in the history of conscientious objection during more than two centuries of American warfare.

Conscientious objection has long been considered part of a male domain that encompasses military conscription and duty. Yet it is clear from the varied contributions of women to Civilian Public Service that some American women have appropriated the conscientious objector role as a model for their own lives, even adopting the legal term "conscientious objector" to describe themselves. As Americans commemorate past wars, such as has occurred recently with fifty-year retrospectives of the Second World War, women's participation in public and private roles invite broad recognition and historical reevaluation.

Many of the women whose stories appear in this book practiced restraint in advocating their right to participate in Civilian Public Service; still, they challenged patriarchal church structures and experimented with new ways to meet family obligations, contribute to the labor force, and provide volunteer services. In so doing they stretched the boundaries of conventional gender role expectations. In subsequent decades these formative experiences in *participating* in social change would also shape their expectations of the daughters and sons they would raise.

During World War II American conscientious objectors hoped their humanitarian responses to suffering would stand as a visible counterpoint to the use of massive force even in what the larger society considered to be a "good war." Looking back, many of them believed they had taken the right path; others were less certain that their participation in Civilian Public Service was the most profound statement they could have made against the war. Regardless, their idealism is remarkable in the context of the cultural pressures they faced. Of the lessons to be drawn from their emerging histories, most fundamental is that on the American home front, pluralistic response, not blindly unified assent, characterized civilian life.

Appendix

Questionnaire on Women and Civilian Public Service

Background

1. What is your date of birth?
2. What has (have) been your life occupation(s)?
3. Education:
   a. Where did you attend high school?
   b. Did you attend college? If so, when and where?
   c. If you attended college, did that experience help to shape your attitudes about war and peace? How so?
   d. Did you do graduate work beyond college? In what field?
4. What was your church affiliation during World War II? What is your present church affiliation?
5. What was your marital status during the war? Date of marriage? What is your marital status now?
6. Did you have children *during* the war? If so, what years and where were they born? If you worked outside the home, who took care of them?
7. Who or what were major influences in your life regarding war and peace (i.e., persons or books)?
8. What were the teachings of your parents on issues of war and peace? Were there differences within your family on these issues?
9. What was the position of your church or minister about issues of war and peace?
10. Although American women were never drafted, Congress debated the issue because of a nursing shortage overseas. Do you remember being aware of this and having opinions about it?
11. World War II is often viewed as a popular war. In your experience, was it a popular war?
12. Where did you work during World War II? Did the war affect your job? How did your coworkers and employers treat you when they identified you with CPS or conscientious objection?

CPS Staff Members

1. Please check as many of the following categories that match your experiences during and immediately after World War II:

    Dietitian on CPS staff

    Nurse on CPS staff

    Member of Women's Voluntary Service Unit ("C.O. Girl")

    Matron on CPS staff

    Relief Training Unit member

2. What were the *years* and *locations* that you served on behalf of CPS? What was your title or position?

3. Describe how you became involved in this work. Who recruited you? What was your motivation for service?

4. What were your primary responsibilities? Did you enjoy your work? What frustrations did you experience?

5. Describe the financial compensation that you received. What kind of salary and benefits, if any, did you have? What other (nonmonetary) rewards existed for the work that you did?

6. Did your work in CPS shape your career or life choices in any way? If so, how?

Wives and Friends of Men in CPS

1. What year was your husband or friend drafted?

2. Did you support his decision to enter CPS? What were your feelings about conscientious objectors?

3. How long was he in CPS?

4. How did his service affect your marriage or relationship?

5. Did he discuss with you his opportunities to transfer to newly opened CPS units, or whether he ought to accept assignments in other geographic areas? What were the major considerations affecting whether or not you moved to be near him?

6. Were you responsible for supporting yourself financially during part or all of the war? Did you support others? Did you experience financial hardships during the war?

7. How supportive were your parents and family members to the conscientious objector stance of your husband or friend? Did he have the support of his church?

8. Did you live near or in any CPS camps/units? If so, where, and under what circumstances? What were your housing arrangements?

9. In communities where you lived, what were the attitudes of people toward conscientious objectors?
10. What churches, if any, did you attend in the communities where you lived? What kinds of attitudes did churchgoers there express toward conscientious objectors?
11. Did you know other women associated with CPS men who also lived in the area? Did you develop friendships with them?
12. Did you participate in any organized activities with other CPS women?

Postwar Experiences

1. How did your home and work situations change when the war ended? Did you return to your home community? What opportunities were open to you?
2. Did you experience any crises or unpleasant encounters related to your associations with Civilian Public Service?
3. What is your most pleasant memory regarding Civilian Public Service?
4. Did your associations with Civilian Public Service help to shape your values in any way? If so, how?
5. Have you been involved in peace activism since World War II (i.e., postwar relief efforts, voluntary service, political work)?
6. Have your children engaged in service or peace witness in recent years? Explain.
7. Have you shared your CPS experiences with others (i.e., attended reunions or written memoirs)?
8. Have you saved diaries, letters, or scrapbooks from CPS?
9. Do you have photographs of women or children in CPS?
10. What lessons do you think pacifists can learn by looking back on World War II and the CPS experience?

Notes

Abbreviations Used in Notes

AMC   Archives of the Mennonite Church, Goshen, Indiana
BHLA Brethren Historical Library and Archives, Elgin, Illinois
DG   Document Group
MLA   Mennonite Library and Archives, North Newton, Kansas
MSHL Menno Simons Historical Library, Harrisonburg, Virginia
NP   Nancy Foster Neumann Papers, Maineville, Ohio
SCPC Swarthmore College Peace Collection, Swarthmore, Pennsylvania

Introduction

1. On the history of conscription in the United States, see Moskos and Chambers, eds., "Conscientious Objectors and the American State." While public policy in the United States has shifted from conscription to voluntarism in the second half of the twentieth century, the phenomenon of conscientious objection persists. The Gulf War prompted an estimated 1,500–2,500 Americans to file claims as C.O.s, and Amnesty International reported that U.S. military officials jailed twenty-nine conscientious objectors illegally during and after the war ("Dellums' Bill," 1).

2. The one hundred thousand figure is an estimate of American male conscientious objectors, ages nineteen to forty-four, who reported for noncombatant service, entered Civilian Public Service, or went to prison. Sibley and Jacob, *Conscription of Conscience*, 84. On noncombatant C.O.s in World War II and the difficulties in estimating their number, see Eller, *Conscientious Objectors and the Second World War*, 28.

3. For a superb bibliographic essay on CPS literature, see Mitchell Robinson, "Civilian Public Service," xiii–xviii. Robinson's dissertation, one of several that assess American conscientious objection during World War II, provides a comprehensive overview of CPS. Earlier histories of CPS include Eisan, *Pathways of Peace*, Gingerich, *Service for Peace*, and Sibley and Jacob, *Conscription of Conscience*. Notable memoirs published in recent years include Zahn, *Another Part of the War*, Dasenbrock, *To the Beat of a Different Drummer*, Waring, *Something for Peace*, Adrian Wilson, *Two Against the Tide*, and van Dyck, *Exercise of Conscience*.

4. The estimate of two thousand women is based upon surveys of the dependents of CPS men, as well as records of women who served as dietitians, nurses, and mental health workers (Sibley and Jacob, *Conscription of Conscience*, 221, 303, Gingerich, *Service for Peace*, 361, and Hershberger, *Mennonite Church in the Second World War*, 184).

5. Quotation from Kreider memo to author.

6. Matt. 5:39.

7. Quoted in Adams, *Peacework*, 186.

8. Chafe, *American Woman*, 136. Chafe published a revised study, *Paradox of Change*, in 1991. By focusing on women's work experiences, D'Ann Campbell, Alan

Clive, Karen Anderson, Ruth Milkman, and others have confirmed the cultural conservatism and gender-typed behavior of the period. See Campbell, *Women at War with America*, 215–38, Clive, "Women Workers in World War II," Anderson, *Wartime Women*, and Milkman, *Gender at Work*. For comparative perspectives on the history of women's wartime labor in Canada and Great Britain, see Pierson, *"They're Still Women After All,"* and Summerfield, "Women, War and Social Change."

9. Di Leonardo, "Morals, Mothers, and Militarism," 601.

10. Elshtain, *Women and War*, 22.

11. Hanley, *Writing War*, 20, 25. See also Higonnet, Jenson, Michel, and Weitz, eds., *Behind the Lines*, 25.

12. Eller, *Conscientious Objectors and the Second World War*, Frazer and O'Sullivan, *"We Have Just Begun to Not Fight,"* Gluck, *Rosie the Riveter Revisited*, and Kesselman, *Fleeting Opportunities*.

13. Fortunately, scholarly work on the interplay of peace history and gender for the pre–World War II period is becoming increasingly sophisticated. On the First World War in particular, see Frances Early's essay, "New Historical Perspectives."

14. Day, "If Conscription Comes for Women," 1. For discussions of Day's radical philosophy in the broader context of World War II pacifism, see Nancy Roberts, *Dorothy Day and the Catholic Worker*, 125, and William Miller, *Dorothy Day*, 345.

15. In 1904 Addams delineated her ideas in an address to the Thirteenth Universal Peace Conference in Boston (Schott, "Women Against War," 1–7).

16. See Joan Hoff Wilson, "Peace is a Woman's Job," 38–53, Bacon, *One Woman's Passion*, and Foster, *The Women and the Warriors*.

17. Gascho, "Experiences During CPS Days." Harriet Hyman Alonso has explored the dissatisfaction and radicalization of some young women of the Vietnam generation who felt that the draft resistance movement exposed their second-class status as citizens. One result was a revival of feminist thought among American peace activists, as Alonso explains in *Peace as a Women's Issue*, 224–26. In the past decade the study of peace history has been enriched by comparative analyses. See Boulding, "Feminist Inventions in the Art of Peacemaking," and two review essays, Frances Early, "New Directions in the Gendered Study of Peace," and Patterson, "Emergence of Peace History."

18. Redekop, "Through the Mennonite Looking Glass," 239.

19. Margaret Taylor Kurtz questionnaire.

20. Margaret Calbeck Neal questionnaire.

21. Joyce Lancaster Wilson questionnaire.

22. Elizabeth Doe Jaderborg questionnaire.

23. Lillian Newell Doucette questionnaire. The best historical account of the U.S. Department of Justice's role in conscientious objectors' appeals is Sibley and Jacob, *Conscription of Conscience*, 53–81.

24. Doris Cline Egge, panel participant in "Women: What It Was Like for Us in CPS Days,"

25. Quoted in Waltner, "Excerpts From the Experiences of a Conscientious Objector," 6.

26. Ibid., 14.

27. Kohn, *Jailed for Peace*, 102–4, 109, note 18. Estimates of the numbers of nonregistrants from 1980 to 1984 range from the Selective Service System's figure

of 382,000, to the General Accounting Office's figure of 700,000. The vast majority of these men escaped prosecution.

28. No comprehensive listing exists for women who took part in Civilian Public Service, but some gaps in the historical record have been filled by the holdings of the Oral History Institute of Bethel College in Kansas. In this collection are more than two hundred interviews with World War II conscientious objectors, including approximately a dozen with women associated with Civilian Public Service. In 1991 and 1992 I conducted sixteen additional interviews with women and deposited these tapes at the Oral History Institute. As a result, data is available from twenty-seven interviews conducted from 1975 to 1992. For a discussion of methodological issues in conducting interviews with veterans and conscientious objectors, see Sprunger and Thiesen, "Mennonite Military Service in World War II," and Eller, "Oral History as Moral Discourse."

29. Photocopies of questionnaire responses have been deposited in the Mennonite Library and Archives, North Newton, Kansas, and the Swarthmore College Peace Collection, Swarthmore, Pennsylvania.

30. Two repositories — the Swarthmore College Peace Collection and the Archives of the Mennonite Church — have begun to solicit the personal papers of women who participated in CPS. Presently, however, few such collections are accessible to researchers, and many journals and letters chronicling C.O.s' experiences remain in attics and closets. For a similar perspective, see Litoff and Smith, eds., *Since You Went Away*, viii–ix.

Chapter One

1. Esko Loewen, "My Work Camp Experience," 9.
2. On the issue of church-state conflict, see Bush, "Military Service, Religious Faith, and Acculturation" and "Drawing the Line," 295–99. Bush argues that among Mennonite groups, the rising numbers of men entering military service signified acculturation to a broadly shared national identity. For estimates of the numbers of objectors who entered military service, see Sibley and Jacob, *Conscription of Conscience*, 86–90, and Sprunger and Thiesen, "Mennonite Military Service in World War II," 481–91.
3. Anna Wiebe Miller questionnaire.
4. Eller, *Conscientious Objectors and the Second World War*, 176.
5. Margaret Calbeck Neal questionnaire response.
6. Wyman, *Paper Walls*, 87, 156–57.
7. Heisey, "They Also Served," 249.
8. Ibid., 118 n. 60. For a discussion of American policy regarding European Jews and the pervasiveness of anti-Semitism in the United States, see Blum, *V Was for Victory*, 172–81.
9. Eller, *Conscientious Objectors and the Second World War*, 176. Religious scholar Gerald Sittser points out the concern and publicity mounted by some Christian leaders about the situation of European Jews but concludes that they "did not succeed in arousing the conscience of the American public, including the Christian public" (Sittser, "Cautious Patriotism," 370).

10. Boyer, "Mennonite and Amish Women in Twentieth-Century North America," 10.

11. Sibley and Jacob, *Conscription of Conscience*, 12–13, Masland et al., "Treatment of the Conscientious Objector," 700–701, and Mitchell Robinson, "Civilian Public Service," 54.

12. Homan, *American Mennonites and the Great War*, 55, 158–59.

13. For a detailed account of the deaths of Joseph Hofer and his brother Michael, also a World War I conscientious objector, see Homan, *American Mennonites and the Great War*, 152–54. Other important sources include Smith, *Coming of the Russian Mennonites*, 276–82, Sibley and Jacob, *Conscription of Conscience*, 15, and Chambers, "Conscientious Objectors and the American State," 33.

14. Gingerich, *Service for Peace*, 27–30. For an early discussion of alternative service, see Hershberger, "Christian's Relation to the State," 20–36.

15. For analyses of World War II rightist women's organizations, see McEnaney, "He-Men and Christian Mothers," and Jeansonne, *Women of the Far Right*. The Women's International League for Peace and Freedom offers a good example of prewar and wartime organizational struggle. For details, see Pois, "U.S. Women's International League for Peace and Freedom," Solomon, "Dilemmas of Pacifist Women," and Bacon, *One Woman's Passion*.

16. Quoted in Heisey, "They Also Served," 254. For male C.O.s' perspectives on Jesus as a moral teacher, see Eller, *Conscientious Objectors and the Second World War*, 94–95.

17. Others included the Socialist Party, the Women's International League for Peace and Freedom, the National Council for the Prevention of War, Fellowship of Reconciliation, the Catholic Worker movement, the Mennonite Central Committee, the Church of the Brethren, the Disciples of Christ, the Federal Council of the Churches of Christ in America, the Seventh Day Adventists, and the Methodist Commission on World Peace (Sibley and Jacob, *Conscription of Conscience*, 46–47). The best overview of the American peace movement's efforts to influence the Burke-Wadsworth legislation is Clifford and Spencer, *First Peacetime Draft*, 126–35, 161, 211–12, 221–23.

18. Fourteen percent of those polled registered no opinion (Cantril, *Public Opinion*, 135).

19. Selective Training and Service Act of 1940, quoted in Gingerich, *Service for Peace*, 437–38.

20. Men who wished to contest their classification had the right to appeal for reclassification by their local draft board (Sibley and Jacob, *Conscription of Conscience*, 71–82, 167).

21. Eller, *Conscientious Objectors and the Second World War*, 32.

22. Kohn, *Jailed for Peace*, 47. On Jehovah's Witnesses in World War II, see also Manwaring, *Render Unto Caesar*, 29–30.

23. Lindner, *Stone Walls and Men*, 302.

24. Esther Eichel, quoted in Hurwitz and Simpson, *Against the Tide*, n.p.

25. Ibid., introduction.

26. Gara, "Road Less Traveled."

27. In 1969 the organization changed its name from the National Service Board for Religious Objectors (NSBRO) to the National Interreligious Service Board for

Conscientious Objectors (NISBCO). For an assessment of the NSBRO and its efforts to assist World War II conscientious objectors, see Wachs, "Conscription, Conscientious Objection, and the Context of American Pacifism," 190–92.

28. Gingerich, *Service for Peace*, 338–44.

29. Ibid., 344; Sibley and Jacob, *Conscription of Conscience*, 292–93; Eller, *Conscientious Objectors and the Second World War*, 31.

30. Keim, *CPS Story*, 110; Gingerich, *Service for Peace*, 63. In addition to these groups and the three historic peace agencies, those affiliated with the National Service Board for Religious Objectors included Assemblies of God, Christadelphian Central Committee, Christadelphian Service Committee, Church of God—Indiana, Church of God—Seventh Day, Congregational Christian Committee for Conscientious Objectors, Department of Social Welfare, Dunkard Brethren Church, Dutch Reformed Church, Episcopal Pacifist Fellowship, Evangelical Church Board of Christian Social Action, Evangelical Mission Covenant, Federal Council Churches of Christ in America, Fellowship of Reconciliation, First Divine Association in America, Central Conference of American Rabbis, Jewish Peace Fellowship, Rabbinical Assembly of America, Augustana Lutheran Fellowship of Reconciliation, Lutheran Peace Fellowship, Megiddo Mission, Molokan Advisory Board, Pacifist Principle Fellowship, Pentecostal Church, Committee on Presbyterians in CPS, Seventh-Day Adventists Committee on National Service and Medical Cadet Training, Unitarian Pacifist Fellowship, United Brethren, War Resisters League, Women's International League for Peace and Freedom, and Young Men's Christian Association (listed in Eller, *Conscientious Objectors and the Second World War*, 44 n. 78). In recent years some of these organizations have planned fiftieth anniversary events commemorating their activism during the Second World War. See, for example, Mary H. Miller's account of the Episcopal Pacifist Fellowship, "Fifty Years of Peacemaking," 14.

31. *Camp Kits*; "Ladies Mend," 2; Rae Hungerford Mason questionnaire. For a transnational perspective on the contributions of churchwomen to war relief, see Gladys Goering, *Women in Search of Mission*, 27–29, and Marlene Epp, "Women in Canadian Mennonite History," 99–100.

32. For the complete list, see "Needs at Civilian Public Service Camps," 15 February 1943, DG 25, Box G-94, "WILPF," SCPC. On the activities of WILPF on behalf of World War II conscientious objectors, see also Nitchie, ed., *W.I.L. in Wartime*.

33. Van Dyck, *Exercise of Conscience*, 5; Ewing, "Pacifist Movement in the Methodist Church," 81.

34. Mrs. Omar Joyce to Albert Gaeddert, 2 March 1942, Gaeddert Papers, MLA-MS-50, Box 1, folder 2, MLA.

35. Ibid.

36. *Mennonite Civilian Public Service Statement of Policy*.

37. Neumann to author, 17 March 1993.

38. *Mennonite Civilian Public Service Camps Bulletin of Information*, 2.

39. Mitchell Robinson, "Civilian Public Service," 238; Keim, "Civilian Public Service: The Moral Equivalent of War," Menno Simons lecture, 29 October 1990, MLA.

40. The only study ever undertaken to assess the socioeconomic and educational backgrounds of CPS assignees remains unpublished: Zahn, "Descriptive Study of Social Backgrounds."

41. See Gingerich, *Service for Peace*, 90, Eller, *Conscientious Objectors and the Second World War*, 50, and Driedger and Kraybill, *Mennonite Peacemaking*, 278 n. 38.

42. Paul Toews, *Mennonites in American Society*, 174. For an assessment of the varied patterns of Mennonite parental and congregational authority, see Kreider, "Environmental Influences," 247–59, 275.

43. Only thirteen denominations had more than 100 members enrolled in CPS, while 449 men listed no church affiliation. "Number of Conscientious Objectors From Each Denomination," in Henry A. Fast Papers, MLA-MS-49, Box 41, folder 361, MLA.

44. Paul Toews argues that Mennonites' understanding of the CPS system differed from other pacifist groups in that they saw it primarily as an act of witness, an "expression of biblical faith" (Toews, *Mennonites in American Society*, 141).

45. Zahn, *Another Part of the War*, 81.

46. Sibley and Jacob, *Conscription of Conscience*, 246–49; see also Beck and Beck, "CPS Protest Songs."

47. Brock, *Twentieth Century Pacifism*, 198.

48. Paul Albrecht to Albert Gaeddert, 23 January 1946, in Gaeddert Papers, MLA-MS-50, Box 3, folder 16, MLA.

49. Mitchell Robinson, "Civilian Public Service," 425.

Chapter Two

1. Higonnet, Jenson, Michel, and Weitz, eds., *Behind the Lines*, 1; Westbrook, " 'I Want a Girl,' " 588–89.

2. Van Gelder, "Men Who Refuse to Fight," 14.

3. Sleater, "C.O. Camp."

4. Stevenson, *Man Called Intrepid*, 111–12. Statistics of World War II American dead and wounded are from U.S. Bureau of the Census, *Historical Statistics of the United States*, pt. 2, 1140.

5. Fussell, *Wartime*, 167–68; Leff, "Politics of Sacrifice," 1296.

6. Quotation from Palmer, "Women's Place in Industry," 23. See also Blum, *V Was for Victory*, 15–52.

7. Wolf, "Women and War Jobs," 212.

8. For a critique of American cultural expectations regarding women's voluntarism, see Campbell, *Women at War with America*, 66–71. On motherhood, see Higonnet, Jenson, Michel, and Weitz, eds., *Behind the Lines*, 154–60. On women's wage work see Higonnet, Jenson, Michel, and Weitz, eds., *Behind the Lines*, 35. On the federal government's role in shaping women's economic and cultural expectations, see Rupp, *Mobilizing Women for War*, and Straub, "United States Government Policy Toward Civilian Women." Robert B. Westbrook in "Fighting for the American Family" has underscored the familial emphases of mobilization rhetoric.

9. Baruch, *You, Your Children, and War*, 154.

10. On the relation of gender to militarism and to pacifist ideology, see Enloe, *Does Khaki Become You?*, 5, 213, and Marlene Epp, " 'United We Stand, Divided We Fall,' " 7.

11. Recently, however, feminist critics within some of these religious communities

have linked conservative social ideology and practice to sexual abuse and domestic violence. For an introduction to the topic see Hildebrand, "Domestic Violence."

12. Fussell, *Wartime*, 167.

13. Quotations from Doris Miller Glick, Esther Lehrman Rinner, and Verda Lambright Kauffman questionnaires.

14. On educational agenda in wartime, see Ronald Cohen, "Schooling Uncle Sam's Children," 47–50, Tuttle, *"Daddy's Gone to War,"* 115–27, and Ugland, "Adolescent Experience," 93–98 and 302–3.

15. Amanda Ediger Bartel questionnaire.

16. Esther Lehrman Rinner questionnaire; see also Margaret Calbeck Neal questionnaire.

17. Esther Lehrman Rinner questionnaire.

18. Ibid.

19. Mildred Morris Gilbert questionnaire.

20. Virginia Krehbiel Kaufman interview with author; Montgomery, "At Peace With Their Choices."

21. William M. Tuttle Jr. addresses the hostility aimed at German American boys and girls in World War II in *"Daddy's Gone to War,"* 180–82. On mob actions against Kansas Mennonites during World War I, see Wedel, *Story of Bethel College*, 236–37, Juhnke, *Vision, Doctrine, War*, 218–28, and Homan, *American Mennonites and the Great War*, 57–98. On the Mennonites' vulnerability in World War II, see Kreider, "Journalist's Private Reflections on the Mennonites," 24.

22. Evelyn Goering Lehman questionnaire.

23. Betty Regier Wasser questionnaire.

24. Zerger interview by Dick. See also Juhnke, *Creative Crusader*, chapter 10, Wedel, *Story of Bethel College*, 420, and Hershberger, *Mennonite Church in the Second World War*, 187.

25. Because of the pressure on school children to participate in financing the war, the Mennonite Central Committee and other peace church organizations arranged for financial institutions to set up savings stamp plans for civilian bond investments. Mennonite Central Committee Peace Section Annual Report, 1943, in Gaeddert Papers, MLA-MS-50, Box 12, folder 97, MLA. For an overview of wartime sales campaigns in American schools, see Ugland, "Adolescent Experience," 93. For an example of criticism of the militarization of public education, see Keesler, "War Financing Through the Schools," 94. On school-sponsored alternatives to the Victory Corps, see Minutes of the Council on Civilian Service, Philadelphia, 25 October 1943, DG 25, Box G-45, "Jacob, Betty," SCPC. For an analysis of the historic peace churches' pre–World War II efforts to create alternative institutions, see Juhnke, "Mennonite Benevolence and Revitalization."

26. Sibley and Jacob, *Conscription of Conscience*, 124. For an overview of wartime news coverage of American C.O.s, see Sareyan, *Turning Point*, 119–28.

27. Frost, "Lew Ayres Case and Conscientious Objection."

28. Stafford, *Down in My Heart*, 47–48.

29. Loewen, ed., *Why I Am a Mennonite*, 186.

30. Zahn, *Another Part of the War*, 81, 92.

31. Stafford, *Down in My Heart*, 28.

32. Detzer, *Appointment on the Hill*, 237.

33. Albert Moorman to Edna and Albert Gaeddert, 17 April 1942, in Gaeddert Papers, MLA-MS-50, Box 1, folder 2, MLA; Virginia Stalter Kreider interview with author.

34. Van Dyck, *Exercise of Conscience*, 76. Historian Marlene Epp has reflected on conscientious objectors' "masculine construction that included patriotism, service, bravery, and support of family" in her provocative study, "Alternative Service and Alternative Gender Roles."

35. Zahn, *Another Part of the War*, 197.

36. Nancy Foster to Thomas B. and Louise Foster, 15 July 1943, NP.

37. Van Dyck, *Exercise of Conscience*, 78–79. On sexual behavior in Civilian Public Service, see Sibley and Jacob, *Conscription of Conscience*, 179; H. H. Brubaker to Henry A. Fast, 19 May 1942, Gaeddert Papers, MLA-MS-50, Box 1, folder 3, MLA; and Vernon Blosser, interview by Kurt Goering, 27 September 1975.

38. Col. Lewis F. Kosch, quoted in "Camper's Manual," Sideling Hill, Pa., March 1942, in Henry A. Fast Papers, MLA-MS-49, Box 40, MLA.

39. H. A. Fast, "Civilian Public Service News," in Henry A. Fast Papers, MLA-MS-49, Box 41, folder 361, MLA.

40. Nancy Foster to Thomas B. and Louise Foster, 24 May 1942, NP.

41. Neumann interview with author, 25 May 1992.

42. Nancy Foster to Thomas B. and Louise Foster, 25 June 1941, NP. See also Gingerich, *Service for Peace*, 229, and Oyer, "Tension and Trouble Beside the 'Deep River,'" 1, 15–19.

43. "Toys to Japanese Create Furor," 29 December 1942, Gaeddert Papers, MLA-MS-50, Box 9, folder 65, MLA. For more on American anti-Japanese sentiment during the war, see Dower, *War Without Mercy*, and Tuttle, *"Daddy's Gone to War,"* 171–73.

44. Kimberly Schmidt, "North Newton WILPF," 10.

45. Kermit Sheets, quoted in Hurwitz and Simpson, *Against the Tide*, n.p.

46. Neumann interview with author.

47. Money, "Analysis of Civilian Public Service Camp Twenty-Seven F," 110–13.

48. On the ironies of conscientious objection and modern warfare, see Juhnke, "Limited War in a Century of Total War," 54.

49. The studies also found that economic status had little impact on one's attitude toward C.O.s. Americans who were under age forty or who had attended college were generally more tolerant of C.O.s (Crespi, "Public Opinion Toward Conscientious Objectors," pts. I–V).

50. Campbell, "Servicewomen of World War II," 257.

51. Westbrook, "'I Want a Girl,'" 605.

Chapter Three

1. Louise Wilson to family members, 5 August 1941, DG 56, Series I, Box 5, "Eugene and Louise Wilson Correspondence," SCPC.

2. Louise Wilson to family members, 29 July 1941, DG 56, Series I, Box 5, Wilson Correspondence, SCPC.

3. Eugene Wilson to family members, 10 August 1941, and Louise Wilson to family members, 5 August 1941, DG 56, Series I, Box 5, Wilson Correspondence, SCPC.

4. Louise Wilson to Mary Lemon, 18 August 1941, DG 56, Series I, Box 5, Wilson Correspondence, SCPC.

5. The U.S. program of unpaid civilian service for conscientious objectors differed from that of other countries. In Canada and Great Britain, government officials assigned conscientious objectors to individual posts in agriculture, forestry, and related fields. As a result, few spouses and friends of C.O.s in those countries had opportunities to relocate near camps. On the status of wives of Canadian conscientious objectors, see Roth, "Conscientious Objection," and Marlene Epp, " 'United We Stand, Divided We Fall.' " On women C.O.s in Great Britain, see Moskos and Chambers, eds., *New Conscientious Objection*, 69, 71, 75–77.

6. Louise Wilson to family members, 6 August 1941, DG 56, Series 1, Box 5, Wilson Correspondence, SCPC.

7. Enloe, *Does Khaki Become You?*, 1, 3, 6, 17. On women as cultural symbols, see also Higonnet, Jenson, Michel, and Weitz, eds., *Behind the Lines*, 160.

8. Norton, *Liberty's Daughters*, 213, 224.

9. Faust, "Altars of Sacrifice," 1213.

10. Pierson, ed., *Women and Peace*, 137–48. Political theorist Jean Bethke Elshtain has identified the "Beautiful Soul" as a metaphor for women and claims that it has long staying power in Western culture: "Pictured as frugal, self-sacrificing, at times delicate, the female Beautiful Soul in time of war has been positioned as a mourner, an occasion for war, and a keeper of the flame of nonwarlike values—and has thus been set up as a being, and a whole way of life, men both cherish and seek to flee, both need and despise" (Elshtain, *Women and War*, 144). On the cultural construction of women in wartime, see also Westbrook, " 'I Want a Girl.' "

11. Meyer, *Journey Through Chaos*, 367. On American female migration in World War II, see Alt and Stone, *Campfollowing*, 98, Chafe, *Paradox of Change*, 125, Terkel, *"Good War,"* 118–19, and Litoff et al., *Miss You*, 68–71; 321–22.

12. Klaw, *Camp Follower*, 34; Litoff et al., *Miss You*, 69–71.

13. Selma D. Unruh questionnaire. On Colorado Springs, consult Abrahams interview with author.

14. Helen Krehbiel Goering questionnaire. On the war's impact on American marriages, see Anderson, *Wartime Women*, 76–77, and Campbell, *Women at War with America*, 8.

15. Ruth Stoltzfus to Grant Stoltzfus, 3 September and 14 September 1944, quoted in Stoltzfus, "Blueberries and Briars." See also Mary Alice Alexander to Howard Alexander, 30 June 1942, DG 56, Series I, Box 5, SCPC, and Marian Garber Leaman questionnaire. On the phenomenon of letter writing, see Hill, *Families Under Stress*, 348, and Litoff and Smith, eds., *Since You Went Away*.

16. DeElda Eicher Hershberger questionnaire.

17. On the history of the legislation, see Alt and Stone, *Campfollowing*, 98, Goldman, "Trends in Family Patterns of U.S. Military Personnel," 123, and Hill, *Families Under Stress*, 359–60. On the reaction of men in CPS, see Werner C. Baum, Report on CPS Regional Conference, Baltimore, Md., 12 December 1943, Gaeddert Papers, MLA-MS-50, Box 3, folder 13, MLA.

18. "Policy Regarding Cases of Dependency of Men in CPS," 30 May 1942, in CPS Vertical File, MLA; Gingerich, *Service for Peace*, 348.

19. Virginia Stalter Kreider interview with author. On population trends during

the war, see Anderson, *Wartime Women*, 76, and May, *Homeward Bound*, 59. On war-time developments in conscription policy, see Flynn, *Draft, 1940–1973*, 73–74.

20. National Service Board for Religious Objectors, "C.O. Dependency," undated pamphlet, in CPS Vertical File, MLA; Mitchell Robinson, "Civilian Public Service," 293.

21. Memo from Ernest Herbster to Irvin Richert et al., 20 December 1945, DG 25, Box A-58, "Men With Children — Statistics," SCPC.

22. Mitchell Robinson, "Civilian Public Service," 295.

23. Ibid., 304.

24. Letter to NSBRO from anonymous assignee, quoted in Sibley and Jacob, *Con-scription of Conscience*, 221–22; Paul Comly French to Anna Wharton Morris, 18 August 1944, DG 25, Box G-52, "Morris, Anna," SCPC.

25. *Experience of the American Friends Service Committee in Civilian Public Service*, 19.

26. Nolt, "CPS Frozen Fund," 206.

27. Quotation from Claude Shotts memo, 2 May 1944, DG 25, Box G-89, SCPC. For a discussion of the ill-fated legislation favored by the National Service Board for Religious Objectors, see Mitchell Robinson, "Civilian Public Service," 279–99. On the fate of the "frozen fund," see Nolt, "CPS Frozen Fund," 206–24, and Frazer and O'Sullivan, "Forgotten Women," 48–49.

28. Albert M. Gaeddert to Henry A. Fast, 4 February 1944, Henry A. Fast Papers, MLA-MS-49, Box 4, folder 28, MLA.

29. "Policy Regarding Cases of Dependency of Men in CPS," 30 May 1942, in CPS Vertical File, MLA; Hershberger, *Mennonite Church in the Second World War*, 80–81.

30. Leland H. Brenneman to Daniel Frysinger, 13 October 1944, DG 25, Box G-25, "Davidson, Lois," and Grace Rhoads to Paul Comly French, 26 March 1944, DG 25, Box G-78, "Rhoads, Grace," both in SCPC.

31. The figures cited for aid delivered by the church agencies and NSBRO to CPS families are from Frazer and O'Sullivan, "Forgotten Women," 48; however, they do not take into account the financial support contributed by other church groups or individuals to families of men in CPS. For a critic's perspective, see Hutchinson, "Wasted Manpower and the C.O.'s," 9.

32. Keim, *CPS Story*, 40; Sibley and Jacob, *Conscription of Conscience*, 124.

33. Barbara Yoder Thomas questionnaire. On CPS weddings, see Stafford, *Down in My Heart*, 47–52, and Brubaker, *Old German Baptists in Civilian Public Service*, 127.

34. Louise Evans to Albert Gaeddert, 24 June 1942, Gaeddert Papers, MLA-MS-50, Box 1, folder 3, MLA.

35. Adrian Wilson, *Two Against the Tide*, 83, 85.

36. Gascho, "Experiences During CPS Days," 1–5.

37. Van Dyck, *Exercise of Conscience*, 228.

38. Betty Bragg Sonnenberg questionnaire.

39. Stafford, *Down in My Heart*, 47.

40. Quotation from Albert Gaeddert to Henry A. Fast, 1 December 1942, Henry A. Fast Papers, MLA-MS-49, Box 3, MLA. See also Jesse Harder to Albert Gaeddert, 10 July 1943, Gaeddert Papers, MLA-MS-50, Box 2, folder 11, MLA, and Charlotte Leap Rutschman questionnaire.

41. Aganetha Fast, "Report — Belton, Montana," 2 October 1944, MCC-CPS Cor-

respondence Files, "Aganetha Fast, 1944," AMC. Fast's assignment followed several months of debate among MCC officials as to how they might best provide leadership to women in CPS. Educators Lois Gunden and Viola Good also traveled in 1944 to more than twenty base camps, relief training programs, and hospital units (Orie O. Miller to Edna Ramseyer, 30 August 1943 and 22 September 1943, MCC-CPS Correspondence Files, "Edna Ramseyer, 1943," Elmer Ediger to Viola Good, 18 April 1944, MCC-CPS Field Records, "Relief Training Schools," Box 2, folder 14, and Aganetha Fast to Albert Gaeddert, 11 September 1944, MCC-CPS Correspondence Files, "Aganetha Fast, 1944," all in AMC).

42. Albert Gaeddert to John M. Reimer, 11 September 1941, Gaeddert Papers, MLA-MS-50, Box 1, folder 1, MLA.

43. Aganetha Fast to Albert Gaeddert, 18 September 1944, MCC-CPS Correspondence Files, "Aganetha Fast, 1944," AMC; Money, "Analysis of Civilian Public Service Camp Twenty-Seven F," 74; Nancy Foster to Thomas B. and Louise Foster, 28 March 1944, NP.

44. Frank Olmstead, "C.P.S. After Eighteen Months — Report of the War Resisters League," 11 November 1942, typescript in Henry A. Fast Papers, MLA-MS-49, Box 40, folder 358, MLA.

45. Ibid.

46. Wilson, *Two Against the Tide*, 126; M. C. Lehman, report on Howard, Pa., camp, undated, H. A. Fast Papers, MLA-MS-49, Box 40, folder 358, and Grant Stoltzfus, Report on Conference of Mennonite CPS Camp Directors, Winona Lake, Ind., 5 August 1942, Gaeddert Papers, MLA-MS-50, Box 9, folder 72, both in MLA.

47. Mitchell Robinson, "Civilian Public Service," 340.

48. Sterling Cole telegram to General Lewis E. Hershey, August 1943, quoted in Mitchell Robinson, "Civilian Public Service," 340.

49. Mitchell Robinson, "Civilian Public Service," 340.

50. Keim, "Civilian Public Service: The Moral Equivalent of War," Menno Simons lecture, 29 October 1990, MLA.

51. Accounts of women who joined C.O. husbands in farm work are in Brubaker, *Old German Baptists in Civilian Public Service*, 128, 160, 183, 210. Salaries and working conditions of C.O. wives working at mental hospitals are discussed in W. Jarrott Harkey to W. M. Hammond Jr., 2 August 1944, "Wives, CPS, Employment," Brethren Service Committee General Subject Files, BHLA; *P.R.N. in a Mental Hospital Community*, 52; Rohrer and Rohrer, *Story of the Lancaster County Conference Mennonites*, 38; and Ralph Buckwalter, Report of Relief Training Unit, 27 October 1945, in *Ypsi Yearbook*.

52. Campbell, *Women at War with America*, 92–96; Elshtain, *Women and War*, 189. As late as 1943, the U.S government actively discouraged mothers of young children from entering the work force, but during the next two years the government took a more flexible position. See Kesselman, *Fleeting Opportunities*, 68.

53. Ruth Krady Lehman questionnaire. On pregnancy in CPS, see also Hernley, "Dietitian's Memoir," 15, and Beth Eldridge Goering questionnaire. After the war, the Mennonite Central Committee compiled and distributed to newly released CPS men a resource book with listings for a wide range of subjects, including family planning. Esko Loewen, "Family and Home," 1945 typescript, CPS Papers, MLA-V-17, folder 77f, MLA.

54. Frances Clayton, panel participant in "Women: What It Was Like for Us in CPS Days."

55. Quoted in van Dyck, *Exercise of Conscience*, 59; see also Melvin F. Funk to Mennonite Central Committee, 30 December 1943, Gaeddert Papers, MLA-MS-50, Box 2, folder 13, MLA.

56. Nancy Foster to Thomas B. Foster and Louise Foster, 1 February 1944, NP.

57. Nice to author.

58. Brubaker, *Old German Baptists in Civilian Public Service*, 130; Mary Morrissett Mullin and Virginia Wright Rohwer questionnaires.

59. Quotation from Gingerich, *Service for Peace*, 379. Also see "Married Men of [CPS Camp No.] 5."

60. *P.R.N. in a Mental Hospital Community*, 66, 70–71; Goering interview with author; Ada Short questionnaire.

61. Emmert to author.

62. Florence Williams Potts questionnaire. C.O. children are discussed in Nancy Foster to Thomas B. Foster, 29 August 1943, NP, and Albert Gaeddert, "Report on Camp Hill City [S.D.]," 17 July 1943, Henry A. Fast Papers, MLA-MS-49, Box 40, folder 358, MLA. On the psychological impact of World War II on American children, see Tuttle, "America's Home Front Children" and *"Daddy's Gone to War."*

63. Pinkerton, "American War Policy Dividing All Classes."

64. Yutzy conversation with author. For a compelling analysis of dress issues among the Mennonites, see Marlene Epp, "Carrying the Banner of Nonconformity."

65. Thanks to Robert S. Kreider for his insights on CPS men's and women's differing experiences. See Kreider, "CPS: A 'Year of Service With Like-Minded Christian Young Men,'" 564.

66. Virginia Wright Rohwer questionnaire.

67. Yutzy conversation with author.

68. LaVaughn Beard questionnaire. On the role of women in CPS mental hospital units, see also Sareyan, *Turning Point*.

69. Morgan to author.

70. Verda De Coursey questionnaire.

71. Margaret Calbeck Neal questionnaire.

72. Virginia Krehbiel Kaufman interview with author.

73. For individual stories of hiring discrimination, see Elma Esau, Pearl Kleinsasser Hofer, Irene Koehn Smith, and Nancy Baker Ewert questionnaires, and Wall interview with author; see also Gomez Letter to Peace Committee of the Western District of the General Conference Mennonite Church. National figures on employment are cited in Hartmann, *Home Front and Beyond*, 102.

74. Mary Alice Alexander to Howard Alexander, 1 June 1942, DG 56, Series I, Box 5, SCPC.

75. Ibid.

76. Virginia Wright Rohwer, Irene Koehn Smith, and Lorene Goering questionnaires.

77. Kathryn Garst Mason, Frieda Schlichting Hiebert, and Florence Wiens questionnaires. Micaela di Leonardo has explored the implications of women's mutual support in "Women's Work, Work Culture, and Consciousness," 494.

78. Nice to author.

Chapter Four

1. Fast interview with author.

2. This estimate of the number of staff women is based on CPS personnel listings, Hiebert Papers, MLA-MS-37, Box 10, folders 71–75 and 140, MLA.

3. Campbell, *Women at War With America*, 66.

4. Neumann to author, 17 March 1993.

5. Some women arrived at their CPS posts with a college education but with little formal training in the tasks to which they were assigned (Gingerich interview with author).

6. Steinson, "Mother Half of Humanity," 275.

7. Swerdlow, *Women Strike for Peace*, 234–35.

8. Lohrenz interview with author.

9. Arthur Gamble to Ed Peacock, 5 February 1944, DG 2, Box 22, "Camps — Medical Staff," SCPC.

10. Estimates of salaries and benefits are based on CPS personnel listings, Hiebert Papers, MLA-MS-37, Box 10, folders 71–75 and 140, and Albert Gaeddert to Rufus M. Franz, 11 October 1943, Gaeddert Papers, MLA-MS-50, Box 2, folder 12, all in MLA.

11. Gomez letter to Peace Committee of the Western District of the General Conference Mennonite Church; J. H. Langenwalter to Henry A. Fast, 13 March 1942, Henry A. Fast Papers, MLA-MS-49, Box 2, folder 16, MLA; Lois Schertz, "CPS Experiences." See also Johnson interview by James Juhnke. For a discussion of how pacifist elementary and secondary school teachers fared during the war, see Sibley and Jacob, *Conscription of Conscience*, 447–50.

12. Showalter, "Being a Camp Dietitian," 1944 speech, in Eby Papers, MSHL.

13. The coeducational AFSC summer work camp program, which began in Europe after World War I and spread to the United States during the 1930s, was an important influence in the development of Civilian Public Service. See Pickett, *For More Than Bread*, 341.

14. Pearl Mierau Janzen questionnaire. See also Hernley, "Dietitian's Memoir," 12; Yoder interview by Krista Yoder; undated listing of candidates for CPS staff, Henry A. Fast Papers, MLA-MS-49, Box 41, folder 360, MLA; and Selma Dick Unruh questionnaire.

15. Gingerich, *Service for Peace*, 312–13; Fast and Spaulding interviews with author.

16. Quote from Henry A. Fast to Aaron J. Claassen, 8 April 1942, Henry A. Fast Papers, MLA-MS-49, Box 3, folder 27, MLA; see also Ina Wiebe to Henry A. Fast, 5 May 1943, Henry A. Fast Papers, MLA-MS-49, Box 3, folder 27, MLA.

17. Newell, *History of the National Nursing Council*, 22, 31.

18. For a summary of the 1943 poll, see Cantril, *Public Opinion*, 1049. On the proposals to conscript women, see Treadwell, *Women's Army Corps*, 95, 247, Alonso, *Peace as a Women's Issue*, 149–51, and Solomon, "Dilemmas of Pacifist Women," 141.

19. Henry A. Fast to Orie O. Miller, 10 September 1942, Henry A. Fast Papers, MLA-MS-49, Box 3, folder 19, MLA.

20. Carol Blosser to Harold S. Bender, 24 November 1942, Bender Papers, Hist. MSS 1–278, file 52, folder 1, AMC.

21. Paul Swett to Mary Newman, 24 March 1942, DG 2, Box 22, "Camps — Medi-

cal Staff," SCPC. On the WMC, see Blum, *V Was for Victory*, 197, and Rupp, *Mobilizing Women for War*, 88.

22. Frances Early, "Foremothers," 148; Nancy Foster to Thomas B. and Louise Foster, 14 January 1943, NP; Lillian Pemberton Willoughby questionnaire. For an overview of the Committee to Oppose the Conscription of Women, see Bacon, *One Woman's Passion*, 226–30.

23. Campbell, "Servicewomen of World War II," 253. The most complete study of the Cadet Nurse Corps remains Beatrice J. Kalisch and Philip A. Kalisch, "From Training to Education: The Impact of Federal Aid on Schools of Nursing in the United States During the 1940s," conducted for the National Institutes of Health in 1972–74. For a summary of this study, see Kalisch and Kalisch, "Cadet Nurse Corps in World War II," 240–42. See also Petry, "U.S. Cadet Nurse Corps," 704–8, Kalisch and Kalisch, *Advance of American Nursing*, 529, and Campbell, *Women at War with America*, 49–61.

24. Reimer interview by Myron Voth.

25. Arthur Gamble to Russ Freeman, 8 June 1943, DG 2, Box 22, "Camps — Medical Staff," SCPC; see also Sibley and Jacob, *Conscription of Conscience*, 167.

26. William Satterwaite to Paul Furnas, 10 December 1942, and Randolph Pyle to Paul Furnas, 8 November 1942, both in DG 2, Box 22, "Camps — Medical Staff," SCPC.

27. Quotation from Arthur Gamble to Ed Peacock, 5 February 1944, DG 2, Box 22, "Camps — Medical Staff," SCPC; see also Gamble to Wilmer Cooper, 22 November 1943, "Camps — Medical Staff," DG 2, Box 22, SCPC.

28. Maude Swartzendruber, one of the association's founders, was eager to train young nurses to combine the professional requirements of nursing, which she defined as intellectual, moral, and physical fortitude, with the spiritual requirement of having a "true Christian experience" (Swartzendruber, "Shall I Be a Nurse?," 427). On the history of the MNA, see Greaser, "Historical Overview of Mennonite Nurses' Association," 177.

29. Driver, "Mennonite Nurses' Association."

30. "Policies of the Mennonite Nurses' Association," 1942, Minute Book, Mennonite Nurses' Association Records, VII-20, AMC.

31. Minutes of May 1944 meeting, Mennonite Nurses' Association Minute Book, VII-20, and Verna M. Zimmerman to Ernest E. Miller, 22 March 1943, MCC-CPS Field Records, file 1, folder 25, both in AMC.

32. Zimmerman interview by Janet Schellenberger.

33. For a discussion of earlier struggles over women's rights in the Mennonite Church, see Klingelsmith, "Women in the Mennonite Church," 180–81.

34. Cantril, *Public Opinion*, 923.

35. Harold S. Bender, "Christian Nurse's Position in Time of War," 1945 typescript, Mennonite Nurses' Association Records, VII-20, Box 3, AMC. See also Bender, "Can a Nonresistant Nurse Serve in the Army?," 7.

36. On the proposals to draft American nurses in 1945, see Nelson, "Nurses for Our Men — The Nation's Womanpower Shortage," 34–35, Treadwell, *Women's Army Corps*, 356, Kalisch and Kalisch, "Women's Draft," 402–13, and Bacon, *One Woman's Passion*, 229–30.

37. Gingerich, *Service for Peace*, 377; Quarterly Report of Camp #85, Howard, R.I., 14 September 1943, MCC-CPS Field Records, file 14, folder 55, AMC.

38. Maurice Early, "Day in Indiana." A fictionalized account of CPS published a generation later supports this perception. In a remote northern California camp setting "the men had been away from their wives and little girls and boys for a long time" and thus could not be expected to say grace before a meal (Habegger, "Little Spoon," 36).

39. Quotation from Albert Gaeddert, report on Three Rivers (Calif.) Camp, 14 August 1943, MCC-CPS Correspondence Files, "Albert Gaeddert, 1943," AMC.

40. Showalter, *Dietitian's Handbook*, 3.

41. Henry A. Fast to Harold S. Bender, 21 May 1941, Bender Papers, Hist. MSS 1–278, Box 52, folder 1, AMC.

42. Schrock interview by Leonard Gross. See also Keiser, "On Cleanliness and Morale," and Harder, "Suggestions for Dormitory Matrons."

43. "Camp Medical Services," 1941 typescript, DG 2, Box 22, "Camps—Medical Staff," SCPC.

44. Paul B. Johnson to James P. Mullin, 2 May 1942, DG 2, Box 22, "Camps—Medical Staff," SCPC; Albert Gaeddert, report on Camp LaPine (Ore.), 21 August 1943, Gaeddert Papers, MLA-MS-50, Box 2, folder 11, MLA. On medical policies for CPS personnel, see "Our Responsibility for Medical Care in Civilian Public Service Camps—Definition of Its Scope and Limitations," 1943 typescript, Henry A. Fast Papers, MLA-MS-49, Box 41, folder 359, MLA.

45. Lohrenz interview with author.

46. Mary M. Mann questionnaire. On deaths in CPS, see *Directory of Civilian Public Service* [1947], xx.

47. Catherine Crocker Harder questionnaire; Reimer interview by Myron Voth; Ellen Harder questionnaire; Moyer diary, entry for 27 July 1943, MSHL. See also Kreider, " 'Good Boys of CPS,' " 5.

48. Arthur Gamble to Edith Ratcliff, 6 October 1944, DG 2, Box 22, "Camps—Medical Staff," SCPC; Henry A. Fast to Marie Lohrenz, 27 August 1943, and Edna M. Peters to Marie Lohrenz, 28 September 1943, both in Lohrenz Papers, MLA-MS-326, MLA.

49. Marie Ediger Widmer questionnaire.

50. "Duties of Dietician," 1941 typescript, DG 2, Box 22, "Dieticians," SCPC; Lillian Pemberton Willoughby questionnaire.

51. Nancy Foster to Thomas B. and Louise Foster, February 1941, NP. For an early account of the Patapsco camp, see Robert E. S. Thompson, "Onward, Christian Soldiers!," 54–55.

52. Neumann to author, 21 June 1992.

53. Nancy Foster to Thomas B. and Louise Foster, April 1944, NP.

54. Nancy Foster to Thomas B. and Louise Foster, 6 June 1943, NP.

55. Hernley, "Dietitian's Memoir," 14. Notable documents related to women's travels in CPS include the 1944 diary of Mary Emma Showalter, in Eby Papers, MSHL the 1944 diary of Aganetha Fast in MLA-MS-47, MLA; Lois Sommer Kreider interview with author; and Edna Quiring Cook Schmidt and Anna Wiebe Miller questionnaires.

56. Elizabeth Hernley to Henry A. Fast, 9 February 1943, MCC-CPS Correspondence Files, IX-6-3, "Elizabeth Hernley, 1943," AMC.

57. Quotation from Hernley, "Dietitian's Memoir," 13. See also Showalter, *Dietician's Handbook*, 10, and Hernley, "Appetites, Rationing, and Camp Dietitians," 6.

58. Quotation from Neumann interview with author; see also Fast interview.

59. Quoted in Litoff and Smith, " 'To the Rescue of the Crops,' " 351.

60. Ibid., 349. For further discussion of women agricultural workers and federal farm policy during World War II, see Jellison, *Entitled to Power*, 131–48.

61. Meal costs depended to some extent on camp size and location. Neumann interview with author; Nancy Foster to Thomas B. and Louise Foster, 17 November 1943, NP; Hernley, "Dietitian's Memoir," 14–15.

62. Hernley, "Dietitian's Memoir," 13–14.

63. On the contributions of the Women's Missionary Association, see Gladys Goering, *Women in Search of Mission*, 27–29, and Women's Missionary Association Papers, MLA-1a-7-B, MLA.

64. Gingerich, *Service for Peace*, 346–47.

65. Westbrook, " 'I Want a Girl,' " 614 n. 21.

66. Showalter diary, entry for 20 March 1944, Eby Papers, MSHL.

67. Nancy Foster to Louise Foster, 1 March 1943, NP.

68. Nancy Foster to Louise Foster, March 1944, NP.

69. Mary Raecher Wiser questionnaire.

70. Wiser to author.

71. Sibley and Jacob, *Conscription of Conscience*, 192.

72. On women's intellectual contributions in CPS settings, see Goossen, "The 'Second Sex,' " 537, and Wilson, *Two Against the Tide*, 120–22.

73. Winifred Beechy interview with author; Virginia Stalter Kreider interview with author.

74. Quotation from Nancy Foster to Louise Foster, 14 July 1941, NP. See also Mary Emma Showalter to Orie O. Miller, 16 December 1943, MCC-CPS Correspondence Files, IX-6-3, "Mary Emma Showalter 1944," AMC.

75. Moyer diary, entries for 30 April and 1 May 1944, MSHL.

76. Albert Gaeddert to Henry A. Fast, 5 December 1942, Henry A. Fast Papers, MLA-MS-49, Box 3, folder 19, MLA.

77. Arthur Gamble to Ed Peacock, 29 January 1945, DG 2, Box 22, "Camps—Medical Staff," SCPC.

78. Showalter diary, entries for 2 February, 23 March, and 8 April 1944, Eby Papers, MSHL.

79. Spaulding interview with author.

80. Lois Keniston Waters and Ruth Rueggeberg Fischer questionnaires.

Chapter Five

1. A few colleges with historic peace church ties abandoned their pacifism during the war and encouraged eligible students to participate in military service. Umble, *Goshen College*, 170. For an overview of military training on American campuses during the war, see Cardozier, *Colleges and Universities in World War II*, 22–49, 135–64.

2. Umble, *Goshen College*, 170.

3. Hostetler letter to CPS friends.

4. Frances Clemens Nyce, panel participant in "Women: What It Was Like for Us in CPS Days."

5. Myrtle L. Molzen to Carl Kreider, 16 May 1943, MCC-CPS Field Records, file 1, folder 25, AMC.

6. Lois Sommer Kreider interview with author. The Women's International League for Peace and Freedom lost 75 percent of its national membership by the end of the war. See Jensen, "When Women Worked," 130, Alonso, *Peace as a Women's Issue*, 146, and Bacon, *One Woman's Passion*, 223.

7. Margaret Calbeck Neal questionnaire.

8. Ibid.

9. Alice Hostetler Loewen Kreider interview with author.

10. Hostetler letter to the editor.

11. Ibid.

12. Bernice Meyer Miller questionnaire.

13. Gingerich, *Service for Peace*, 306–8; Sibley and Jacob, *Conscription of Conscience*, 188.

14. Umble, *Goshen College*, 171; Dasenbrock, *To the Beat of a Different Drummer*, 68.

15. Applications of women who were interested in relief training in 1943 are in MCC-CPS Field Records, file 1, folder 25, AMC.

16. Selma Dick Unruh questionnaire.

17. Dasenbrock, *To the Beat of a Different Drummer*, 69; Crill to author.

18. The fate of the China Unit is detailed in Mitchell Robinson, " 'Healing the Bitterness of War and Destruction,' " 24–48. See also Brock, *Twentieth Century Pacifism*, 188, Eller, *Conscientious Objectors and the Second World War*, 31, Sibley and Jacob, *Conscription of Conscience*, 228, and Gingerich, *Service for Peace*, 307–8.

19. Paul Toews, *Mennonites in American Society*, 129.

20. Ellen Harder questionnaire.

21. Dasenbrock, *To the Beat of a Different Drummer*, 85; Gingerich, *Service for Peace*, 308–10; Lehman, "Program of the M.C.C. to Train Relief Workers."

22. Historian Robert Kreider has used the term "continuing education" to describe short-term service programs in postwar Europe. See Kreider's "Impact of MCC Service on American Mennonites," 248.

23. Edna Ramseyer Kaufman interview by Kurt Goering; Elmer Ediger, "Beginnings of Voluntary Service," 5.

24. Constitution of the COGs, 12 August 1943, in Hiebert Papers, MLA-MS-37, Box 15, folder 141, MLA. The term "C.O. Girl" appeared in CPS camp publications as early as September 1942, although women advocates of Civilian Public Service did not organize formally until almost a year later.

25. Minutes of COGs meeting, 14 August 1943, in Hiebert Papers, MLA-MS-37, Box 15, folder 141, MLA.

26. Blanche Spaulding et al., "Preliminary Statement, Women's Volunteer Service," 1943 typescript, DG 25, Box G-94, "Women's Draft," SCPC.

27. Minutes of COGs meeting, 14 August 1943, in Hiebert Papers, MLA-MS-37, Box 15, folder 141, MLA.

28. Minutes of cogs meeting, 13 August 1943, in Hiebert Papers, MLA-MS-37, Box 15, folder 141, MLA.

29. Minutes of cogs meeting, 14 August 1943, in Hiebert Papers, MLA-MS-37, Box 15, folder 141, MLA.

30. Minutes of meeting of the MCC Executive Committee, 19 August 1943, Mennonite Central Committee Papers, MLA-V-1, MLA.

31. Orie O. Miller to Edna Ramseyer, 22 September 1943, MCC-CPS Correspondence Files, "Edna Ramseyer [1943]," AMC.

32. Doris Miller Glick questionnaire; Edna Ramseyer Kaufman interview by Kurt Goering. In 1944, CPS official Warren Leatherman reported that the new women's unit at Howard, Rhode Island, had "boosted morale 100%" ("Quarterly Report, CPS Unit at State Hospital, Howard, R.I.," 15 June 1944, MCC-CPS Field Records, file 14, folder 55, AMC).

33. Edna Ramseyer Kaufman interview.

34. The estimate of three hundred female college-age recruits for Civilian Public Service is derived from reports in Gingerich, *Service for Peace*; "Women Serve in Mental Hospitals" pamphlet (Elgin, Ill.: Brethren Service Committee, 1945), in Brethren Service Committee General Subject Files, "Women's Work," BHLA; and "Women's Service in Mental Hospitals" pamphlet (Byberry, Pa.: Philadelphia State Hospital, 1944), in Civilian Public Service Vertical File, MLA.

35. Initially, Mennonite CPS officials planned to charge a fee to women to cover administrative and educational expenses. But they decided against that plan in favor of absorbing costs as part of their overall relief training budget, in recognition "of the contribution which these women are making even to the men's side of the whole relief training set-up" (Ernest E. Miller to Orie O. Miller, 16 March 1944, MCC-CPS Field Records, file 2, folder 10, AMC).

36. Gingerich, *Service for Peace*, 213–14; Sareyan, *Turning Point*, 62; and Laura Fitzsimmons, "Report of a Survey in Nursing in Mental Hospitals in the U.S. and Ontario, Canada," ca. 1943, both in DG 2, Box 36c, "Women's Service," SCPC.

37. "CPS Women at Work," *Rhythms* newsletter, September 1943, p. 6, DG 2, Box Publications/Camp #49, "Philadelphia State Hospital," SCPC.

38. "Women's Civilian Public Service Unit" flier and Anna Gray Morris memo to Carol Richie, 6 October 1943, DG 25, Box Sp 16, "Women's CPS," SCPC.

39. Miles, "Memories of Philadelphia State Hospital," 19. A three-page, undated listing of the duties expected of CPS attendants in mental health work is contained in the Gaeddert Papers, MLA-MS-50, Box 9, folder 64, MLA.

40. *The Attendant*, which in 1946 was expanded and renamed *The Psychiatric Aide*, was a project of the NSBRO. See also "Conscientious Way," and Sareyan, *Turning Point*, 130–34, 147–48. On educational opportunities for women in CPS, see Carl Kreider to Registrar of Bethel College, 14 July 1944, Bethel College — P. S. Goertz Papers, folder 62, and "Women's Service in Mental Hospitals" pamphlet, CPS Vertical File, both in MLA.

41. Quotation from Roosevelt, "If You Ask Me," 38. For her newspaper column remarks, see "Conscientious Objectors Want to Be Useful," and "Objectors are Not Same Type Citizens as the Fighting Men," 34. Follow-up correspondence includes Paul Comly French to Eleanor Roosevelt, DG 25, Box G-79, "Eleanor Roosevelt,"

scpc. The finest analysis of Roosevelt's role in the dependency controversy is Frazer and O'Sullivan's "Forgotten Women," 48–49. On her visit to the Poughkeepsie institution, see Betty Regier Wasser and Lois Meyer King questionnaires.

42. Sareyan, *Turning Point*, 93–94.

43. Walter Lerch, a journalist with the *Cleveland Press*, was the first to publish stories about the conscientious objectors' efforts to improve conditions for mentally ill Ohioans. See "*Life* Hails Press Exposé of Mentally Ill Care," and Albert Q. Maisel, "Bedlam 1946." For individual reports of patient abuse and neglect, see "Women's Service Unit—Cleveland, Applications and Evaluations," mcc-cps Data Files, IX-12, 1, amc. An overview of the Cleveland State Hospital scandal is in Sareyan, *Turning Point*, 66–71.

44. Bartel interview by Kurt Goering.

45. Esther Lehrman Rinner questionnaire.

46. Miles, "Memories of Philadelphia State Hospital," 19.

47. Lois Meyer King questionnaire.

48. Warren Leatherman, "Quarterly Report—C.P.S. Unit #85," 15 June 1944, mcc-cps Field Records, file 14, folder 55, amc; Gingerich, *Service for Peace*, 229.

49. Ruth Dingman, "In Service of the Forgotten," unpublished article, 1943, in DG 2, Box 36c, "Women's Service," scpc.

50. Unruh, *Study of Service Programs*, 88, 94. See also Oyer, "Reflections of a 'C.O. Girl,'" 4–7.

Chapter Six

1. The three were Hazel Senner, Stella Waltner, and Amanda Ediger. Buhler to author.

2. In 1945 and 1946, a yearning for normalcy was evident among cps men and women who looked forward to pursuing long-deferred educational and career goals. Observers noted that married cps assignees were turning attention toward their own affairs and taking a less active role in the community life of Civilian Public Service, and that pregnancy was on the rise at units where wives were living with their husbands. Dasenbrock, *To the Beat of a Different Drummer*, 139.

3. See, for example, Dorothy Thompson, "New Woman in the New America," 6. Most Americans viewed the wartime pattern of women working outside the home as temporary and assumed that the majority of women workers would return to domestic settings when veterans returned. Ironically, although World War II offered unprecedented opportunities for redefining gender roles, Americans in the immediate postwar period were eager to normalize family relations as an antidote to the domestic disruptions of the war years (Anderson, *Wartime Women*, 111, Clive, "Women Workers in World War II," and Campbell, *Women at War with America*, 237–38). See also Hartmann, *Home Front and Beyond*, 224–25.

4. Mae Richard Alliman questionnaire.

5. Ruth Krady Lehman questionnaire. Historian Paul S. Boyer offers an account of how fear and anxiety permeated American life after August 6, 1945, in *By the Bomb's Early Light*, ch. 1.

6. Carol Zens Kellam to John Kellam, 11 August 1945, quoted in Litoff and Smith,

eds., *Since You Went Away*, 227. John Kellam was released from prison in November 1946.

7. Nancy Foster to Thomas B. and Louise Foster, April 1944, NP.

8. In addition, the church agencies responsible for administering Civilian Public Service developed strategies to assist men as they were released. The AFSC, BSC, MCC, and NSBRO offered personal and vocational counseling, assistance in job placement, and emergency loans. Patterning their efforts after the GI Bill, the agencies also offered modest grants-in-aid for men wishing to attend colleges, technical schools, or graduate programs and arranged for cooperating colleges to give applicants exams and academic credit for work completed while in Civilian Public Service (Mitchell Robinson, "Civilian Public Service," 431–32; and "Rehabilitation Plans of M.C.C. and Various Mennonite Conference Groups," 1946, Bethel College — Edmund G. Kaufman Presidential Papers, MLA-111-1a 1g, folder 113, "E. G. Kaufman," "Memorandum on Demobilization as it Pertains to Mennonite Colleges," [1945], in Henry A. Fast Papers, MLA-MS-49, Box 41, folder 360, and "Job Opportunities for Ex-CPS Men," *CPS Bulletin*, 4 April 1946, in Gaeddert Papers, MLA-MS-50, Box 9, folder 65, all in MLA). On postwar educational opportunities for ex-CPS men, see Hershberger, *Mennonite Church in the Second World War*, 85–86.

9. "Local Committees to Aid Discharged Conscientious Objectors," Bulletin #18 of the Interagency Demobilization Committee, 18 October 1945, Bethel College — Edmund G. Kaufman Presidential Papers, MLA-111-1a 1g, folder 13, "E. G. Kaufman," MLA.

10. Voth, "Education for C.P.S. Men," 10.

11. Henry A. Fast to Katherine Derksen, 18 July 1944, Henry A. Fast Papers, MLA-MS-49, Box 4, folder 35, MLA.

12. "Weekly News Notes," 6 June 1945, Women's Missionary Association Papers, MLA-1a-7-B, folder 64, MLA.

13. James W. Cannon, Judge Advocate General of the Veterans of Foreign Wars, 27 June 1945, quoted in Mitchell Robinson, "Civilian Public Service," 440.

14. Mitchell Robinson, "Civilian Public Service," 448.

15. Dasenbrock, *To the Beat of a Different Drummer*, 139.

16. Several factors contributed to this inequity in the federal government's treatment of conscientious objectors. Most importantly, veterans' groups continued to pressure federal officials not to be too lenient. In addition, during the months immediately following the war, some hospital administrators and farmers who had been benefiting from C.O. labor expressed concern about a continuing shortage of workers willing to take low-paying jobs in mental health and agriculture. These employers lobbied for a continuation of the CPS "detached service" arrangements that provided C.O. workers to hospitals and farms (Mitchell Robinson, "Civilian Public Service," 468–71).

17. "C.O.'s at Md. U."

18. By March 1946 these pressures resulted in the withdrawal of the American Friends Service Committee from CPS administration. A number of other agencies also terminated their support, including the Association of Catholic Conscientious Objectors, the Commission on World Peace of the Methodist Church, the Episcopal Pacifist Fellowship, and the American Baptist Home Mission Association. Both the Mennonite Central Committee and Brethren Service Committee also considered

pulling out of CPS, but after learning that the federal government intended to take charge of the camps and units formerly administered by the other agencies, they decided to continue operating their share of the program until conscription came to an end (Mitchell Robinson, "Civilian Public Service," 460–65; "Should the Mennonite Church Continue CPS?" [1945], typescript in Hiebert Papers, MLA-MS-37, Box 15, folder 141, MLA).

19. For an analysis of the CPS walkouts, see Sibley and Jacob, *Conscription of Conscience*, 336–39, and Mitchell Robinson, "Civilian Public Service," 479–88.

20. Sibley and Jacob, *Conscription of Conscience*, 388–98. On the Gallup poll, see Cantril, *Public Opinion*, 135.

21. On the prospect of American postwar military training, see Muste, "Shall We Have Universal Military Training?," 98, 112, and "Report of the Subcommittee on C.P.S. Policy," 3 November 1944, in Minutes Book (1925–44), Peace Problems Committee Records, "Orie O. Miller," I-3-5.3, AMC. Most who followed these debates assumed that in the future, required government service would affect men, not women. In 1950, Congress did briefly consider conscripting women after President Truman endorsed the idea of requiring national registration of women for defense purposes. But military advisers familiar with the history of the Women's Army Corps counseled against drafting women, and the issue lay dormant until the Vietnam War. See Treadwell, *Women's Army Corps*, 759.

22. In mainstream religious and intellectual circles during the middle to late 1940s, American pacifists' denunciations of military policy generally fell on deaf ears. As an illustration, see Paul Boyer's discussion of A. J. Muste's 1947 book *Not by Might* in *By the Bomb's Early Light*, 219–21.

23. Quoted in Shank and Shank, *Our Boys in Civilian Public Service*, 28.

24. Menno Fast, "CPS Research," *Constructive Peace Service*, 28 December 1946, in Gaeddert Papers, MLA-MS-50, Box 9, folder 65, MLA.

25. *Directory of Civilian Public Service* (1947). A revised and updated version of the *Directory*, with names of some C.O. spouses and women who participated as administrative staff, was published in 1994.

26. Evelyn Cook Dick Schmidt, Verda De Coursey, and Geraldine Rugg Braden questionnaires. On sexual polarization in the immediate postwar period, see Hartmann, "Prescriptions for Penelope," 224, 236.

27. Virginia Jenney Drury questionnaire.

28. See Elshtain and Tobias, eds., *Women, Militarism, and War*, 117, Gluck, *Rosie the Riveter Revisited*, xi, and Kesselman, *Fleeting Opportunities*, 123.

29. Joyce Lancaster Wilson, Kathryn Garst Mason, Isabel Mount Miller, Margaret Hope Bacon, Elizabeth Doe Jaderborg, and Lois Meyer King questionnaires; Hernley to author.

30. Hernley, quoted in Jalane Schmidt, "Women in CPS," 307. See also Hernley, "Dietitian's Memoir," 12–17.

31. Charlotte Leap Rutschman questionnaire.

32. Isabel Mount Miller questionnaire.

33. LaVaughn Hansen Beard questionnaire.

34. Brown, *Loyalty and Security*, 95; telephone conversation with Mae Alliman, Iowa City, 3 October 1994.

35. Elizabeth Goering, "Four Decades of Writing the Circle Letter!," 4.

36. Ibid.

37. Adaline Pendleton Satterthwaite questionnaire.

38. Yutzy conversation with author.

39. LaVaughn Hansen Beard questionnaire.

40. Joyce Lancaster Wilson and Mary Raecher Wiser questionnaires.

41. Verda De Coursey questionnaire. For a discussion of the dilemmas of conscientious objectors, see Pickett, *For More Than Bread*, 334.

42. Margaret Calbeck Neal questionnaire.

43. Maribel Brands Todd questionnaire.

44. LaVaughn Hansen Beard questionnaire. See also the discussion of anti-Semitism in Eller, *Conscientious Objectors and the Second World War*, 174–75.

45. Verda Lambright Kauffman questionnaire.

46. Mary Elizabeth Lehman Handrich questionnaire. For another perspective on wives' wartime experiences as breadwinners, see Marlene Epp, "Alternative Service and Alternative Gender Roles."

47. Elizabeth Shetler Barge questionnaire.

48. Ruth Krady Lehman questionnaire.

49. Isabel Mount Miller questionnaire.

50. Ruth Krady Lehman, quoted in Myers, "Valiant Soldiers for Peace," 20.

51. Lois Schertz, "CPS Experiences," 1. See also Barbara Yoder Thomas and Esta Miller Hershberger questionnaires.

52. Analysis based on the responses of sixty-eight women who replied to the question: "Have your children engaged in service or peace witness in recent years? Explain."

53. Catherine Harder Crocker questionnaire.

54. Lillian Wenger Sommer, Imogene Porter Hanawalt, and Viola Zehr King questionnaires; see also Shapiro, ed., *History of National Service in America*, 22.

55. Morgan to author.

56. Pearl Mierau Janzen questionnaire.

57. Detzer, *Appointment on the Hill*, 252.

Conclusion

1. Quotation from Elshtain, *Women and War*, 139.

Bibliography

Unpublished Materials

Archival Collections

Elgin, Illinois
  Brethren Historical Library and Archives
    Brethren Service Committee General Subject Files
Goshen, Indiana
  Archives of the Mennonite Church
    Bender, Harold S. Hist. MSS 1–278
    Mennonite Central Committee — Civilian Public Service Field Records
      (IX-13-1), Correspondence Files (IX-6-3), and Data Files (IX-12, #1-7)
    Mennonite Nurses' Association Records, VII-20
    Peace Problems Committee Records, I-3-5
Harrisonburg, Virginia
  Menno Simons Historical Library
    Eby, Mary Emma Showalter. Personal Papers
    Moyer, Bessie. Diary (photocopy). September 12, 1942–May 3, 1944
Maineville, Ohio
  Neumann, Nancy Foster. Personal Papers. Photocopies in the author's possession
North Newton, Kansas
  Mennonite Library and Archives
    Bethel College — Edmund G. Kaufman Presidential Papers
    Bethel College — P. S. Goertz Papers
    Civilian Public Service Papers, MLA-V-17
    Civilian Public Service Vertical File
    Fast, Aganetha, Papers, MLA-MS-47
    Fast, Henry A., Papers, MLA-MS-49
    Gaeddert, Albert, Papers, MLA-MS-50
    Hiebert, P. C., Papers, MLA-MS-37
    Keim, Albert N., "Civilian Public Service and World War II," 39th series in the
      Menno Simons Lectureship, October 28–30, 1990. Tape recordings of five
      lectures
    Lohrenz, Marie, Papers, MLA-MS-326
    Mennonite Central Committee Papers, MLA-V-1
    Women's Missionary Association Papers, MLA-1a-7-B
Swarthmore, Pennsylvania
  Swarthmore College Peace Collection
    American Friends Service Committee — Civilian Public Service Records.
      Document Group #2
    Civilian Public Service — Personal Papers and Collected Materials. Document
      Group #56
    Friends Committee on National Legislation Records. Document Group #47

National Interreligious Service Board for Conscientious Objectors Records. Document Group #25

Manuscripts

Bender, John. "The Role of Mennonite Women Volunteers in Civilian Public Service During World War II: A Thesis Proposal." Associated Mennonite Biblical Seminaries, Elkhart, Ind., 1981.

Boyer, Paul. "Mennonite and Amish Women in Twentieth-Century North America." Paper presented at the annual meeting of the Organization of American Historians, Washington, D.C., April 1995.

Buhler, Hazel Senner. Letter to the author, 4 January 1993.

Crill, Helene B. Letter to the author, 6 September 1992.

Driver, Evelyn J. "The Mennonite Nurses' Association, 1942–1978." The University of Virginia, 1984.

Emmert, Elsie. Letter to the author, 13 May 1991.

Epp, Marlene. "Alternative Service and Alternative Gender Roles: Conscientious Objectors in B.C. During World War II." Paper presented at the BC and Beyond: Gender Histories Conference, University of Victoria, British Columbia, June 1994.

Fast, Aganetha. "What I Have Found in Civilian Public Service." 1945. Mennonite Library and Archives, North Newton, Kans.

Frost, Jennifer. "The Lew Ayres Case and Conscientious Objection." Paper presented at the annual meeting of the Organization of Historians, Chicago, 3 April 1992.

Gara, Larry. "The Road Less Traveled: War Resisters in World War II." Paper presented at the World War II: 1944 — A Fifty-Year Perspective Conference, Siena College, Loudonville, New York, 3 June 1994.

Gascho, Elva F. "Experiences During CPS Days." 1981. Photocopy in the author's possession.

Gomez, Florence Marie Auernheimer. Letter to Peace Committee of the Western District of the General Conference Mennonite Church, 16 November 1990. Photocopy in the author's possession.

Harder, Ellen. "Suggestions for Dormitory Matrons." Undated handwritten notes. Photocopy in the author's possession.

Hernley, Elizabeth Sieber. Letter to the author, 1 April 1991.

Keeney, William. "Civilian Public Service and Related World War II Experiences." 1971. Mennonite Library and Archives, North Newton, Kans.

Kreider, Robert S. Memo to the author, 7 June 1993.

Morgan, Mary Bruce. Letter to the author, 20 August 1994.

Myers, Karen L. "Valiant Soldiers for Peace: Mennonite Women and Civilian Public Service During World War II." Eastern Mennonite College, 1992.

Neumann, Nancy Foster. Letters to the author, 21 June 1992 and 17 March 1993.

Nice, Luella. Letter to the author, 15 April 1991.

Oyer, Vance Gordon. "Civilian Public Service, Mennonite Benevolence, and an American Identity." Paper presented at Illinois History Symposium, 6–7 December 1991.

Schertz, Lois. "CPS Experiences." 1991. Photocopy in the author's possession.

Stoltzfus, Ruth Brunk. "Blueberries and Briars." 1991 typescript, Harrisonburg, Va. Privately held.

Waltner, Edward J. B. "Excerpts From the Experiences of a Conscientious Objector in the First World War." 1942 typescript. Mennonite Library and Archives, North Newton, Kans.

Wiser, Mary. Letter to the author, 31 March 1994.

Dissertations and Theses

Bush, Perry. "Drawing the Line: American Mennonites, the State, and Social Change, 1935–1973." Ph.D. diss., Carnegie Mellon University, 1990.

Cummins, Dorris. "Civilian Public Service Unit Sixty-Three: Mennonite Conscientious Objectors in World War II." M.A. thesis, Florida Atlantic University, 1982.

Etten, Thomas James. "An Historical and Ethical Evaluation of Selective Conscientious Objection in the United States." Ph.D. diss., Catholic University of America, 1970.

Ewing, E. Keith. "The Pacifist Movement in the Methodist Church During World War II: A Study of Civilian Public Service in a Nonpacifist Church." M.A. thesis, Florida Atlantic University, 1982.

Grimsrud, Theodore Glenn. "An Ethical Analysis of Conscientious Objection to World War II." Ph.D. diss., Graduate Theological Union, 1988.

Kirk, Robert. "Hey Kids! The Mobilization of American Children in the Second World War." Ph.D. diss., University of California, Davis, 1991.

Money, Edward L., Jr. "An Analysis of Civilian Public Service Camp Twenty-Seven F, Orlando, Florida." M.A. thesis, Florida Atlantic University, 1975.

Robinson, Mitchell Lee. "Civilian Public Service During World War II: The Dilemmas of Conscience and Conscription in a Free Society." Ph.D. diss., Cornell University, 1990.

Schott, Linda Kay. "Women Against War: Pacifism, Feminism, and Social Justice in the United States, 1915–1941." Ph.D. diss., Stanford University, 1985.

Sittser, Gerald L., Jr. "A Cautious Patriotism: The American Churches and the Second World War." Ph.D. diss., University of Chicago, 1989.

Ugland, Richard M. "The Adolescent Experience as a Case Study." Ph.D. diss., Indiana University, 1977.

Wachs, Theodore R. "Conscription, Conscientious Objection, and the Context of American Pacifism, 1940–1945." Ph.D. diss., University of Illinois, 1976.

Zahn, Gordon. "A Descriptive Study of the Social Backgrounds of Conscientious Objectors in Civilian Public Service During World War II." Ph.D. diss., Catholic University of America, 1953.

Interviews

Abrahams, Ethel. Interview with author. North Newton, Kans., 9 February 1991. Tape recording, Mennonite Library and Archives, North Newton, Kans.

Bartel, Amanda Ediger. Interview by Kurt Goering, 10 May 1976. Tape recording, Mennonite Library and Archives, North Newton, Kans.

Beechy, Winifred. Interview with author. Goshen, Ind., 9 March 1991. Tape recording, Mennonite Library and Archives, North Newton, Kans.

Blosser, Vernon. Interview by Kurt Goering, 27 September 1975. Tape recording, Mennonite Library and Archives, North Newton, Kans.

Fast, Naomi Brubaker. Interview with author. Goessel, Kans., 17 July 1992. Tape recording, Mennonite Library and Archives, North Newton, Kans.

Gaeddert, Albert and Edna. Interview with author. North Newton, Kans., 9 February 1991. Tape recording, Mennonite Library and Archives, North Newton, Kans.

Gingerich, Shirley. Interview with author. Goshen, Ind., 9 March 1991. Tape recording, Mennonite Library and Archives, North Newton, Kans.

Goering, Elizabeth. Interview with author. Moundridge, Kans., 23 February 1991. Tape recording, Mennonite Library and Archives, North Newton, Kans.

Groff, Thelma Miller. Interview with author. Goshen, Ind., 9 March 1991. Tape recording, Mennonite Library and Archives, North Newton, Kans.

Hershberger, Clara. Interview with author. Goshen, Ind., 9 March 1991. Tape recording, Mennonite Library and Archives, North Newton, Kans.

Johnson, Selma Rich Platt. Interview by James Juhnke, 25 January 1975. Tape recording, Mennonite Library and Archives, North Newton, Kans.

Kaufman, Edna Ramseyer. Interview by Kurt Goering, 27 April 1976. Tape recording, Mennonite Library and Archives, North Newton, Kans.

Kaufman, Virginia Krehbiel. Interview with author. McPherson, Kans., 17 July 1992. Tape recording, Mennonite Library and Archives, North Newton, Kans.

Kreider, Alice Hostetler Loewen. Interview with author. Goshen, Ind., 9 March 1992. Tape recording, Mennonite Library and Archives, North Newton, Kans.

Kreider, Lois Sommer. Interview with author. North Newton, Kans., 6 August 1992. Tape recording, Mennonite Library and Archives, North Newton, Kans.

Kreider, Virginia Stalter. Interview with author. Goshen, Ind., 9 March 1991. Tape recording, Mennonite Library and Archives, North Newton, Kans.

Lohrenz, Marie. Interview with author. Mountain Lake, Minn., 2 March 1991. Tape recording, Mennonite Library and Archives, North Newton, Kans.

Neumann, Nancy Foster. Interview with author. Maineville, Ohio, 25 May 1992. Tape recording, Mennonite Library and Archives, North Newton, Kans.

Reimer, Selma. Interview by Myron Voth, 16 January 1976. Tape recording, Mennonite Library and Archives, North Newton, Kans.

Schrock, Alta. Transcript of interview by Leonard Gross, 19 January 1990. Hist. MSS 6–241, Archives of the Mennonite Church, Goshen, Ind.

Sheehan, Arthur. Transcript of interview by John Kelley. 1962. Dorothy Day — Catholic Worker Collection, Series W-9, Box 2, Marquette University Archives, Memorial Library, Milwaukee, Wis.

Spaulding, Blanche. Interview with author. North Newton, Kans., 8 February 1991. Tape recording, Mennonite Library and Archives, North Newton, Kans.

Wall, Marie Loepp. Interview with author. Buhler, Kans., 20 July 1992. Tape recording, Mennonite Library and Archives, North Newton, Kans.

"Women: What It Was Like for Us in CPS Days." Tape recording of women panelists at CPS reunion in New Windsor, Md., September 1990. Tape recording in possession of Hazel Peters, New Windsor, Md.

Yoder, Katie. Interview by Krista Yoder, December 1989. Tape recording, Mennonite Library and Archives, North Newton, Kans.

Yutzy, Rose Weirich. Conversation with author. Goshen, Ind., 10 March 1991. Notes in the author's possession.

Zerger, Karolyn Kaufman. Interview by Daagya S. Dick, 7 October 1989. Tape recording, Mennonite Library and Archives, North Newton, Kans.

Zimmerman, Verna. Interview by Janet Schellenberger, 25 November 1987. Hist. MSS 6–281, Archives of the Mennonite Church, Goshen, Ind.

Published Materials

Books and Pamphlets

Adams, Judith Porter. *Peacework: Oral Histories of Women Peace Activists*. Boston: Twayne, 1991.

Alonso, Harriet Hyman. *Peace as a Women's Issue: A History of the U.S. Movement for World Peace and Women's Rights*. Syracuse: Syracuse University Press, 1993.

———. *The Women's Peace Union and the Outlawry of War, 1921–1942*. Knoxville: University of Tennessee Press, 1989.

Alt, Betty Sowers, and Bonnie Domrose Stone. *Campfollowing: A History of the Military Wife*. New York: Praeger, 1991.

Anderson, Karen. *Wartime Women: Sex Roles, Family Relations, and the Status of Women During World War II*. Westport, Conn.: Greenwood Press, 1981.

Bacon, Margaret Hope. *One Woman's Passion for Peace and Freedom: The Life of Mildred Scott Olmsted*. Syracuse: Syracuse University Press, 1993.

Baruch, Dorothy W. *You, Your Children, and War*. New York: D. Appleton-Century, 1942.

Blum, John Morton. *V Was for Victory: Politics and American Culture During World War II*. New York: Harcourt Brace Jovanovich, 1976.

Boyer, Paul. *By the Bomb's Early Light: American Thought and Culture at the Dawn of the Atomic Age*. New York: Pantheon Books, 1985.

Brock, Peter. *Twentieth Century Pacifism*. New York: Van Nostrand Reinhold, 1970.

Brown, Ralph S., Jr. *Loyalty and Security: Employment Tests in the United States*. New Haven: Yale University Press, 1958.

Brubaker, John W. *Old German Baptists in Civilian Public Service*. West Alexandria, Ohio: John W. Brubaker, 1989.

Campbell, D'Ann. *Women at War With America: Private Lives in a Patriotic Era*. Cambridge: Harvard University Press, 1984.

Camp Kits. Akron, Pa.: Mennonite Central Committee, 1941.

Cantril, Hadley. *Public Opinion, 1935–1946*. Princeton: Princeton University Press, 1951.

Cardozier, V. R. *Colleges and Universities in World War II*. Westport, Conn.: Praeger, 1993.

Chafe, William Henry. *The American Woman: Her Changing Social, Economic, and Political Roles, 1920–1970*. New York: Oxford University Press, 1972.

———. *The Paradox of Change: American Women in the Twentieth Century*. New York: Oxford University Press, 1991.

Chidester, Ann. *No Longer Fugitive*. New York: Charles Scribner's Sons, 1943.

Civilian Public Service #91: Mansfield State Training School and Hospital. N.p.: Mansfield CPS Alumni, 1956.

Clifford, J. Garry, and Samuel R. Spencer Jr. *The First Peacetime Draft*. Lawrence: University Press of Kansas, 1986.

Coles, Robert. *The Call of Service: A Witness to Idealism*. Boston: Houghton Mifflin, 1993.

Cott, Nancy F. *The Grounding of Modern Feminism*. New Haven: Yale University Press, 1987.

Dasenbrock, J. Henry. *To the Beat of a Different Drummer: A Decade in the Life of a World War II Conscientious Objector*. Winona, Minn.: Northland Press, 1989.

DeBenedetti, Charles. *The Peace Reform in American History*. Bloomington: Indiana University Press, 1980.

Detour . . . Main Highway: Our CPS Stories. Goshen, Ind.: College Mennonite Church, 1995.

Detzer, Dorothy. *Appointment on the Hill*. New York: Henry Holt and Co., 1948.

Directory of Civilian Public Service, May 1941 to March 1947. Washington, D.C.: National Service Board for Religious Objectors, [1947].

Directory of Civilian Public Service, May 1941 to March 1947. Rev. and updated. Washington, D.C.: National Interreligious Service Board for Conscientious Objectors, 1994.

Dower, John W. *War Without Mercy: Race and Power in the Pacific War*. New York: Pantheon, 1986.

Driedger, Leo, and Donald B. Kraybill. *Mennonite Peacemaking: From Quietism to Activism*. Scottdale, Pa.: Herald Press, 1994.

Eisan, Leslie. *Pathways of Peace: A History of the Civilian Public Service Program Administered by the Brethren Service Committee*. Elgin, Ill.: Brethren Publishing House, 1948.

Eller, Cynthia. *Conscientious Objectors and the Second World War: Moral and Religious Arguments in Support of Pacifism*. New York: Praeger, 1991.

Elshtain, Jean Bethke. *Women and War*. New York: Basic Books, 1987.

Elshtain, Jean Bethke, and Sheila Tobias, eds. *Women, Militarism, and War*. Savage, Md.: Rowman and Littlefield, 1990.

Enloe, Cynthia. *Does Khaki Become You?: The Militarisation of Women's Lives*. London: Pluto Press, 1983.

Epp, Frank H. *Mennonites in Canada, 1920–1940: A People's Struggle for Survival*. Toronto: Macmillan of Canada, 1982.

Evans, Sara. *Personal Politics: The Roots of Women's Liberation in the Civil Rights Movement*. New York: Knopf, 1979.

The Experience of the American Friends Service Committee in Civilian Public Service. Philadelphia: American Friends Service Committee, 1945.

Fiftieth Anniversary — Reunion, Akron Headquarters Staff of Civilian Public Service Years 1941–1946. Akron, Pa.: Mennonite Central Committee, 1992.

Flynn, George Q. *The Draft, 1940–1973*. Lawrence: University Press of Kansas, 1993.

Foster, Carrie A. *The Women and the Warriors: The U.S. Section of the Women's International League for Peace and Freedom, 1915–1946*. Syracuse: Syracuse University Press, 1995.

Frazer, Heather T., and John O'Sullivan. *"We Have Just Begun to Not Fight": An Oral History of Conscientious Objectors in Civilian Public Service During World War II*. New York: Twayne, 1996.

Fussell, Paul. *Wartime: Understanding and Behavior in the Second World War*. New York: Oxford University Press, 1989.

Gingerich, Melvin. *Service for Peace: A History of Mennonite Civilian Public Service*. Akron, Pa.: Mennonite Central Committee, 1949.

Gluck, Sherna Berger. *Rosie the Riveter Revisited: Women, the War, and Social Change*. Boston: Twayne, 1987.

Goering, Gladys V. *Women in Search of Mission: A History of the General Conference Mennonite Women's Organization*. Newton, Kans.: Faith and Life Press, 1980.

Hanley, Lynne. *Writing War: Fiction, Gender, and Memory*. Amherst: University of Massachusetts Press, 1991.

Hartmann, Susan. *The Home Front and Beyond: American Women in the 1940s*. Boston: Twayne, 1982.

Hershberger, Guy F. *The Mennonite Church in the Second World War*. Scottdale, Pa.: Mennonite Publishing House, 1951.

Hicks, Granville. *Behold Trouble*. New York: Macmillan, 1944.

Higonnet, Margaret R., Jane Jenson, Sonya Michel, and Margaret Weitz, eds. *Behind the Lines: Gender and the Two World Wars*. New Haven: Yale University Press, 1987.

Hill, Reuben. *Families Under Stress: Adjustment to the Crises of War Separation and Reunion*. New York: Harper, 1949.

Homan, Gerlof D. *American Mennonites and the Great War, 1914–1918*. Scottdale, Pa.: Herald Press, 1994.

Hurwitz, Deena, and Craig Simpson. *Against the Tide: Pacifist Resistance in the Second World War*. New York: War Resisters League, 1984.

Janzen, William. *Limits on Liberty: The Experience of Mennonite, Hutterite, and Doukhobor Communities in Canada*. Toronto: University of Toronto Press, 1990.

Jeansonne, Glen. *Women of the Far Right: The Mothers' Movement and World War II*. Chicago: The University of Chicago Press, 1996.

Jellison, Katherine. *Entitled to Power: Farm Women and Technology, 1913–1963*. Chapel Hill: University of North Carolina Press, 1993.

Juhnke, James C. *Creative Crusader: Edmund G. Kaufman and Mennonite Community*. North Newton, Kans.: Bethel College, 1994.

———. *Vision, Doctrine, War: Mennonite Identity and Organization in America, 1890–1930*. Scottdale, Pa.: Herald Press, 1989.

Kalisch, Philip A., and Beatrice J. Kalisch. *The Advance of American Nursing*. Boston: Little, Brown, 1986.

Kauffman, J. Howard, and Leo Driedger. *The Mennonite Mosaic: Identity and Modernization*. Scottdale, Pa.: Herald Press, 1991.

Keim, Albert N. *The CPS Story: An Illustrated History of Civilian Public Service*. Intercourse, Pa.: Good Books, 1990.

Keim, Albert N., and Grant M. Stoltzfus. *The Politics of Conscience: The Historic Peace Churches and America at War, 1917–1955*. Scottdale, Pa.: Herald Press, 1988.

Kesselman, Amy. *Fleeting Opportunities: Women Shipyard Workers in Portland and Vancouver During World War II and Reconstruction*. Albany: State University of New York Press, 1990.

Kessler-Harris, Alice. *Out to Work: A History of Wage-Earning Women in the United States.* New York: Oxford University Press, 1982.

Klaw, Barbara. *Camp Follower: The Story of a Soldier's Wife.* New York: Random House, 1943.

Klippenstein, Lawrence. *That There Be Peace: Mennonites in Canada and World War II.* Winnipeg: Manitoba C.O. Reunion Committee, 1979.

Kohn, Stephen M. *Jailed for Peace: The History of American Draft Law Violators, 1658–1985.* Westport, Conn.: Greenwood Press, 1986.

Leed, Eric J. *No Man's Land: Combat and Identity in World War I.* Cambridge: Cambridge University Press, 1979.

Lindner, Robert M. *Stone Walls and Men.* New York: Odyssey Press, 1946.

Litoff, Judy Barrett, et al. *Miss You: The World War II Letters of Barbara Wooddall Taylor and Charles E. Taylor.* Athens: University of Georgia Press, 1990.

Litoff, Judy Barrett, and David C. Smith, eds. *Since You Went Away: World War II Letters from American Women on the Home Front.* New York: Oxford University Press, 1991.

———. *We're in This War Too: World War II Letters from American Women in Uniform.* New York: Oxford University Press, 1994.

Loewen, Harry, ed. *Why I am a Mennonite.* Scottdale, Pa.: Herald Press, 1988.

Lummis, Trevor. *Listening to History: The Authenticity of Oral Evidence.* London: Hutchinson, 1987.

Manwaring, David R. *Render Unto Caesar: The Flag-Salute Controversy.* Chicago: University of Chicago Press, 1962.

Mason, Rae Hungerford. *The Inimitable George Mason.* Centralia, Wash.: Rae Hungerford Mason, 1991.

May, Elaine Tyler. *Homeward Bound: American Families in the Cold War Era.* New York: Basic Books, 1988.

MCC-CPS Camp Manual. Akron, Pa.: Mennonite Central Committee, 1942.

Mennonite Central Committee, Akron, Pa.: Fiftieth Anniversary — Reunion. Akron, Pa.: Reunion Planning Committee, 1992.

Mennonite Civilian Public Service Camps Bulletin of Information. Akron, Pa.: Mennonite Central Committee, 1941.

Mennonite Civilian Public Service Statement of Policy. Akron, Pa.: Mennonite Central Committee, 1943.

Mennonite Women's Relief Activities Letter. Akron, Pa.: Mennonite Central Committee, December 1943.

Meyer, Agnes E. *Journey Through Chaos.* New York: Harcourt, Brace and Co., 1944.

Milkman, Ruth. *Gender at Work: The Dynamics of Job Segregation by Sex During World War II.* Chicago: University of Illinois Press, 1987.

Miller, William D. *Dorothy Day: A Biography.* San Francisco: Harper and Row, 1982.

Moskos, Charles C., and John Whiteclay Chambers II, eds. *The New Conscientious Objection: From Sacred to Secular Resistance.* New York: Oxford University Press, 1993.

Newell, Hope. *The History of the National Nursing Council.* N.p.: National Organization of Public Health, 1952.

Nitchie, Elizabeth, ed. *The W.I.L. in Wartime.* Philadelphia: Women's International League for Peace and Freedom, 1943.

Norton, Mary Beth. *Liberty's Daughters: The Revolutionary Experience of American Women, 1750–1800.* Boston: Little, Brown, 1980.

On the Edge of the War Zone: Women Writers and World War I. Tulsa: University of Tulsa, 1990.

Pickett, Clarence E. *For More Than Bread.* Boston: Little, Brown, 1953.

Pierson, Ruth Roach. *"They're Still Women After All": The Second World War and Canadian Womanhood.* Toronto: McClelland and Stewart, 1986.

——, ed. *Women and Peace: Theoretical, Historical, and Practical Perspectives.* London: Croom Helm, 1987.

P.R.N. in a Mental Hospital Community. Marlboro, N.J.: Publications Committee, [1946].

Reverby, Susan M. *Ordered to Care: The Dilemma of American Nursing, 1850–1945.* Cambridge: Cambridge University Press, 1987.

Roberts, Mary M. *American Nursing: History and Interpretation.* New York: Macmillan, 1954.

Roberts, Nancy. *Dorothy Day and the Catholic Worker.* Albany: State University of New York Press, 1984.

Rohrer, Peter L., and Mary E. Rohrer. *The Story of the Lancaster County Conference Mennonites in Civilian Public Service.* N.p., 1946.

Rupp, Leila J. *Mobilizing Women for War: German and American Propaganda, 1939–1945.* Princeton: Princeton University Press, 1978.

Sareyan, Alex. *The Turning Point: How Men of Conscience Brought About Major Change in the Care of America's Mentally Ill.* Washington, D.C.: American Psychiatric Press, 1994.

Shank, Luke J., and James M. Shank. *Our Boys in Civilian Public Service of the Washington Co., Md./Franklin Co., Pa. Conference.* Chambersburg, Pa.: Luke and James Shank, 1947.

Shapiro, Peter, ed. *A History of National Service in America.* College Park, Md.: University of Maryland Center for Political Leadership and Participation, 1994.

Showalter, Mary Emma. *Dietitian's Handbook for Mennonite Civilian Public Service Camps.* Akron, Pa.: Mennonite Central Committee, 1944.

Sibley, Mulford Q., and Philip E. Jacob. *Conscription of Conscience: The American State and the Conscientious Objector, 1940–1947.* Ithaca: Cornell University Press, 1952.

Smith, C. Henry. *The Coming of the Russian Mennonites.* Berne, Ind.: Mennonite Book Concern, 1927.

Socknat, Thomas P. *Witness Against War: Pacifism in Canada 1900–1945.* Toronto: University of Toronto Press, 1987.

Stafford, William E. *Down in My Heart.* Elgin, Ill.: Brethren Press, 1947.

Stevenson, William. *A Man Called Intrepid.* New York: Harcourt Brace Jovanovich, 1976.

Swartzendruber, Maude. *The Lamp in the West.* LaJunta, Colo.: LaJunta Mennonite School of Nursing, 1975.

Swerdlow, Amy. *Women Strike for Peace: Traditional Motherhood and Radical Politics in the 1960s.* Chicago: University of Chicago Press, 1993.

Taylor, Stanley. *Activities of the Pacifist Conscript.* N.p., 1946.

Terkel, Studs. *"The Good War": An Oral History of World War II.* New York: Pantheon Books, 1984.

Thorne, Barrie, ed. *Rethinking the Family: Some Feminist Questions.* New York: Longman, 1982.

Toews, J. A. *Alternative Service in Canada During World War II*. Winnipeg: The Christian Press, 1959.

Toews, Paul. *Mennonites in American Society, 1930–1970: Modernity and the Persistence of Religious Community*. Scottdale, Pa.: Herald Press, 1996.

Treadwell, Mattie. *The Women's Army Corps*. Washington, D.C.: Office of Military History, 1954.

Tuttle, William M., Jr. *"Daddy's Gone to War": The Second World War in the Lives of America's Children*. New York: Oxford University Press, 1993.

Umble, John. *Goshen College, 1894–1954*. Goshen, Ind.: Goshen College, 1955.

Unruh, Wilfred J. *A Study of Service Programs*. Elkhart, Ind.: Associated Mennonite Biblical Seminaries, 1965.

U.S. Bureau of the Census. *Historical Statistics of the United States, Bicentennial Edition*. Washington, D.C.: U.S. Government Printing Office, 1975.

Van Dyck, Harry. *Exercise of Conscience: A World War II Objector Remembers*. Buffalo, N.Y.: Prometheus Books, 1990.

The Voice of Peace. Hill City, S.D.: Civilian Public Service Camp #57, 1946.

Wagler, David, and Roman Raber. *The Story of the Amish in Civilian Public Service*. Boonsboro, Md.: David Wagler, 1945.

Waring, Thomas. *Something for Peace: A Memoir*. Hanover, N.H.: Thomas Waring, 1989.

Wedel, Peter J. *The Story of Bethel College*. North Newton, Kans.: Bethel College, 1954.

Wenger, Roy, ed. *CPS Smokejumpers 1943 to 1946: Life Stories*. Vols. 1 and II. Missoula: The author, 1990, 1991.

Williamson, Janice, and Deborah Gorham. *Up and Doing: Canadian Women and Peace*. Toronto: The Women's Press, 1989.

Wilson, Adrian. *Two Against the Tide: A Conscientious Objector in World War II*. Austin: W. Thomas Taylor, 1990.

Wittner, Lawrence. *Rebels Against War: The American Peace Movement, 1941–1960*. New York: Columbia University Press, 1969.

Wyman, David S. *Paper Walls: America and the Refugee Crisis, 1938–1941*. Amherst: University of Massachusetts Press, 1968.

Ypsi Yearbook. Ypsilanti, Mich.: Publication Committee, 1946.

Zahn, Gordon. *Another Part of the War: The Camp Simon Story*. Amherst: University of Massachusetts Press, 1979.

Articles

Beck, Vincent, and Ervin Beck. "CPS Protest Songs." *Mennonite Life* 51 (December 1996): 14–25.

Bender, Harold S. "Can a Nonresistant Nurse Serve in the Army?" *Mennonursing* 1 (March 1945): 7.

Boals, Kay. "Some Reflections on Women and Peace." *Peace and Change* 1 (Spring 1973): 56–59.

Boulding, Elise. "Feminist Inventions in the Art of Peacemaking." *Peace and Change* 20 (October 1995): 408–38.

Brumberg, Joan Jacobs, and Nancy Tomes. "Women in the Professions: A Research

Agenda for American Historians." *Reviews in American History* 10 (June 1982): 275–96.

Bush, Perry. "Military Service, Religious Faith, and Acculturation: Mennonite GIs and Their Church, 1941–1945." *Mennonite Quarterly Review* 67 (July 1993): 261–82.

———. " 'We Have Learned to Question Government.' " *Mennonite Life* 45 (June 1990): 13–17.

Campbell, D'Ann. "Servicewomen of World War II." *Armed Forces and Society* 16 (Winter 1990): 251–70.

Clive, Alan. "Women Workers in World War II: Michigan as a Test Case." *Labor History* 20 (1979): 44–72.

Cohen, J. "Women in Peace and War." In *Psychological Factors of Peace and War*, edited by Tom H. Pear, 91–110. New York: The Philosophical Library, 1950.

Cohen, Ronald D. "Schooling Uncle Sam's Children: Education in the USA, 1941–1945." In *Education and the Second World War*, edited by Roy Lowe, 46–58. London: Falmer Press, 1992.

"The Conscientious Way." *Time*, 6 January 1946.

Cook, Blanche Wiesen. "Feminism and Peace Research: Thoughts on Alternative Strategy." *Women's Studies Quarterly* 12 (Summer 1984): 18–19.

Corwin, E. P. "Mennonites Bear Expenses of Henry Objectors' Camp." *Peoria Star*, 5 April 1942.

"C.O.'s at Md. U." *Washington Daily News*, 2 April 1946.

Crespi, Leo P. "Public Opinion Toward Conscientious Objectors and Some of Their Psychological Correlates." *Journal of Psychology* 18 (July 1944): 81–117.

———. "Public Opinion Toward Conscientious Objectors: II. Measurement of National Approval-Disapproval." *Journal of Psychology* 19 (April 1945): 209–50.

———. "Public Opinion Toward Conscientious Objectors: III. Intensity of Social Rejection in Stereotype and Attitude." *Journal of Psychology* 19 (April 1945): 251–76.

———. "Public Opinion Toward Conscientious Objectors: IV. Opinions on Significant CO Issues." *Journal of Psychology* 19 (April 1945): 277–310.

———. "Public Opinion Toward Conscientious Objectors: V. National Tolerance, Wartime Trends, and the Scapegoat Hypothesis." *Journal of Psychology* 20 (October 1945): 321–46.

Davenel, George F. "When Johnny Comes Marching Home." *Independent Woman* 24 (July 1945): 182–83, 201.

Day, Dorothy. "Forty-Eight Women Will Not Register." *The Catholic Worker* 9 (December 1942): 1, 3.

———. "If Conscription Comes for Women." *The Catholic Worker* 10 (January 1943): 1.

"Dellums' Bill to Strengthen Military C.O. Process," *The Reporter for Conscience' Sake* 49 (April 1992): 1.

Di Leonardo, Micaela. "Morals, Mothers, and Militarism: Antimiltarism and Feminist Theory." *Feminist Studies* 11 (Fall 1985): 599–617.

———. "Women's Work, Work Culture, and Consciousness." *Feminist Studies* 11 (Fall 1985): 490–95.

Early, Frances. "Foremothers: An Interview With Mildred Scott Olmsted." *Atlantis: Women's Studies Journal* 12 (Fall 1986): 143–51.

——. "New Directions in the Gendered Study of Peace, Social Violence, Militarism, and War." *Journal of Women's History* 6 (Spring 1994): 75–86.

——. "New Historical Perspectives on Gendered Peace Studies." *Women's Studies Quarterly* 23 (Fall/Winter 1995): 22–31.

Early, Maurice. "The Day in Indiana." *Indianapolis Star*, 28 August 1941.

Ediger, Elmer. "The Beginnings of Voluntary Service." *MCC Report* (Winter 1959): 4–7.

Eller, Cynthia. "Oral History as Moral Discourse." *Oral History* 18 (Spring 1990): 45–75.

Epp, Marlene. "Alternative Service and Alternative Gender Roles: Conscientious Objectors in B.C. During World War II." *BC Studies* (Spring/Summer 1995): 139–58.

——. "Carrying the Banner of Nonconformity: Ontario Mennonite Women and the Dress Question." *Conrad Grebel Review* 8 (Fall 1990): 237–57.

——. "'United We Stand, Divided We Fall': Canadian Mennonite Women as COs in World War II." *Mennonite Life* 48 (September 1993): 7–10.

——. "Women in Canadian Mennonite History: Uncovering the 'Underside.'" *Journal of Mennonite Studies* 5 (1987): 90–107.

Faust, Drew Gilpin. "Altars of Sacrifice: Confederate Women and the Narratives of War." *Journal of American History* (March 1990): 1200–1228.

Frazer, Heather T., and John O'Sullivan. "Forgotten Women of World War II: Wives of Conscientious Objectors in Civilian Public Service." *Peace and Change* 5 (Fall 1978): 46–51.

"Free the War Objectors!" *The Christian Century* 62 (10 October 1945): 1150–51.

Gildersleeve, Virginia C. "Women Must Help Stop Wars." *Women's Home Companion*, May 1945, 32.

Goering, Elizabeth. "Four Decades of Writing the Circle Letter!" *Wichita NOW Times*, November 1990, 4.

Goldman, Nancy L. "Trends in Family Patterns of U.S. Military Personnel During the 20th Century." In *The Social Psychology of Military Service*, edited by Nancy L. Goldman and David R. Segal. London: Sage Publications, 1976.

Goossen, Rachel Waltner. "The 'Second Sex' and the 'Second Milers': Mennonite Women and Civilian Public Service." *Mennonite Quarterly Review* 66 (October 1992): 525–38.

Gray, Gladys. "Women and Friends CPS." *Friends Journal* 38 (January 1992): 18–19.

Greaser, Frances Bontrager. "A Historical Overview of Mennonite Nurses Association." In *The Gift of Presence*, edited by Dave Jackson, Neta Jackson, and Beth Landis, 177–79. Scottdale, Pa.: Herald Press, 1991.

Habegger, Alfred. "A Little Spoon." *New Yorker*, 11 January 1982, 34–39.

Hartmann, Susan. "Prescriptions for Penelope: Literature on Women's Obligations to Returning World War II Veterans." *Women's Studies* 5 (1978): 223–39.

Heisey, Mary Jane. "They Also Served: Brethren in Christ Women and Civilian Public Service." *Brethren in Christ History and Life* 18 (August 1995): 228–71.

Hernley, Elizabeth Sieber. "Appetites, Rationing, and Camp Dietitians." *The Mennonite*, July 1943, 5–7.

———. "A Dietitian's Memoir." *Mennonite Life* 46 (September 1991): 12–17.

Hershberger, Guy F. "The Christian's Relation to the State in Time of War: Is Alternative Service Desirable and Possible?" *Mennonite Quarterly Review* 9 (January 1935): 20–36.

Hildebrand, Mary Anne. "Domestic Violence: A Challenge to Mennonite Faith and Peace Theology." *Conrad Grebel Review* 10 (Winter 1992): 73–79.

Hostetler, Alice. Letter to cps friends. *Deep River Echo* 1, no. 11 (September 1942).

Hutchinson, Dorothy L. "Wasted Manpower and the C.O.'s." *The Progressive*, 16 July 1945, 9.

James, William. "The Moral Equivalent of War." *McClure's Magazine*, August 1910.

Jensen, Joan M. "When Women Worked." *California History* 67 (June 1988): 118–31.

Juhnke, James C. "Limited War in a Century of Total War." In *Weathering the Storm: Christian Pacifist Responses to War*, edited by Susan Janzen, 53–59. Newton, Kans.: Faith and Life Press, 1991.

———. "Mennonite Benevolence and Revitalization in the Wake of World War I." *Mennonite Quarterly Review* 60 (January 1986): 15–30.

Kalisch, Beatrice J., and Philip A. Kalisch, "The Cadet Nurse Corps in World War II." *American Journal of Nursing* 76 (February 1976): 240–42.

———. "The Women's Draft: An Analysis of the Controversy Over the Nurses' Selective Service Bill of 1945." *Nursing Research* 22 (September/October 1973): 402–13.

Keesler, Don C. "War Financing Through the Schools." *School and Society* 60 (5 August 1944): 94.

Keiser, Mrs. Ora M. "On Cleanliness and Morale." *Deep River Echo* 1, no. 10 (August 1942).

Klassen, Pamela. "What's Bre(a)d in the Bone: The Bodily Heritage of Mennonite Women." *Mennonite Quarterly Review* 68 (April 1994): 229–47.

Klingelsmith, Sharon. "Women in the Mennonite Church, 1900–1930." *Mennonite Quarterly Review* 54 (July 1980): 163–207.

Kreider, Robert S. "cps: A 'Year of Service With Like-Minded Christian Young Men': cps Camp No. 5, Colorado Springs, Colorado, 1941–42." *Mennonite Quarterly Review* 66 (October 1992): 546–79.

———. "Environmental Influences Affecting the Decisions of Mennonite Boys of Draft Age." *Mennonite Quarterly Review* 16 (October 1942): 247–59, 275.

———. "The 'Good Boys of cps.'" *Mennonite Life* 46 (September 1991): 4–11.

———. "The Impact of mcc Service on American Mennonites." *Mennonite Quarterly Review* 44 (July 1970): 245–61.

———. "A Journalist's Private Reflections on the Mennonites." *Mennonite Life* 45 (June 1990): 18–25.

"The Ladies Mend." *Deep River Echo* 1, no. 11 (September 1942).

Leff, Mark H. "The Politics of Sacrifice on the American Home Front in World War II." *Journal of American History* 77 (March 1991): 1296–1318.

"Legislation." *The Reporter*, 15 March 1945, 4.

Lehman, M. C. "The Program of the M.C.C. to Train Relief Workers." *Mennonite Weekly Review*, 20 January 1944.

"*Life* Hails Press Exposé of Mentally Ill Care." *The Cleveland Press*, 4 May 1946.

Litoff, Judy Barrett, and David C. Smith. " 'To the Rescue of the Crops': The Women's Land Army During World War II." *Prologue* 25 (Winter 1993): 346–59.

Loewen, Esko. "My Work Camp Experience," *The Mennonite*, 25 March 1941, 9.

Ludlow, Peter W. "The International Protestant Community in the Second World War." *Journal of Ecclesiastical History* 29 (July 1978): 311–62.

McEnaney, Laura. "He-Men and Christian Mothers: The America First Movement and the Gendered Meanings of Patriotism and Isolationism." *Diplomatic History* 18 (Winter 1994): 47–57.

Maisel, Albert Q. "Bedlam 1946." *Life*, 6 May 1946.

"The Married Men of [CPS Camp No.] 5." *Pike View Peace News* 4 (January 1945): 6.

Masland, John W., et al. "Treatment of the Conscientious Objector Under the Selective Service Act of 1940." *American Political Science Review* 36 (August 1942): 697–701.

Mellown, Muriel. "One Woman's Way to Peace: The Development of Vera Brittain's Pacifism." *Frontiers* 8 (1985): 2–6.

Miles, Alice Calder. "Memories of Philadelphia State Hospital." *Friends Journal* (January 1992): 19.

Miller, Mary H. "Fifty Years of Peacemaking." *The Witness* 72 (November 1989): 14.

Montgomery, Alan. "At Peace With Their Choices." *The Hutchinson (Kans.) News*, 30 May 1993, 1, 3.

————. "Soldiers of Peace." *The Hutchinson (Kans.) News*, 7 December 1991, 10.

Mosemann, Orpah. "The Mennonite Nurses' Association," *Gospel Herald*, 22 June 1948, 591–92.

Muste, A. J. "Shall We Have Universal Military Training?" *Independent Woman* 24 (July 1945): 98, 112.

Nelson, Josephine. "Nurses for Our Men — The Nation's Womanpower Shortage." *Independent Woman* 24 (February 1945): 34–35, 50–52.

"New Directory of CPS in Progress," *The Reporter for Conscience' Sake* 48 (August 1991): 3.

Nolt, Steve. "The CPS Frozen Fund: The Beginning of Peace-time Interaction Between Historic Peace Churches and the United States Government." *Mennonite Quarterly Review* 67 (April 1993): 201–24.

Norton, Mary Beth. "Eighteenth Century American Women in Peace and War: The Case of the Loyalists." *William and Mary Quarterly*, 3rd. ser., 33 (July 1976): 386–409.

"Objectors Relieve Ypsilanti Hospital." *Detroit News*, 2 April 1943.

Oyer, Vance Gordon. "Reflections of a 'C.O. Girl' — Fern Grieser Massanari." *Illinois Mennonite Heritage* 18 (March 1991): 4–7.

————. "Tension and Trouble Beside the 'Deep River': CPS Camp #22 at Henry." *Illinois Mennonite Heritage* 18 (March 1991): 1, 15–19.

Palmer, Gladys. "Women's Place in Industry." *Current History* 6 (January 1944): 19–24.

Patterson, David S. "The Emergence of Peace History," *Reviews in American History* 23 (1995): 139–36.

Penner, Carol. "Mennonite Women's History: A Survey." *Journal of Mennonite Studies* 9 (1991): 122–35.

Petry, Lucile. "U.S. Cadet Nurse Corps." *American Journal of Nursing* 43 (August 1943): 704–8.

Pinkerton, William. "American War Policy Dividing All Classes." *Washington Evening Star*, 22 September 1941.

Pois, Anne Marie. "The U.S. Women's International League for Peace and Freedom and American Neutrality, 1935–1939." *Peace and Change* 14 (July 1989): 263–84.

Ramseyer, Edna. "Will Ye Heed the Call?" *Missionary News and Notes* 18 (November 1943): 1.

Redekop, Magdalene. "Through the Mennonite Looking Glass." In *Why I am a Mennonite: Essays in Mennonite Identity*, edited by Harry Loewen, 226–52. Scottdale, Pa.: Herald Press, 1988.

"Reflections on My CPS Experience." *Gospel Herald*, 24 May 1966, 469.

Robinson, Jo Ann. "Women, War and Resistance to War: A Transnational Perspective." *Peace and Change* 4 (Fall 1977): 8.

Robinson, Mitchell L. " 'Healing the Bitterness of War and Destruction': CPS and Foreign Service." *Quaker History* 85 (Fall 1996): 24–48.

Roosevelt, Eleanor. "Conscientious Objectors Want to Be Useful." *Philadelphia Record*, 21 June 1944.

———. "If You Ask Me." *Ladies Home Journal*, June 1944, 38.

———. "Objectors are Not Same Type Citizens as the Fighting Men." *Washington Daily News*, 21 June 1944, 34.

Roth, Lorraine. "Conscientious Objection: The Experiences of Some Canadian Mennonite Women During World War II." *Mennonite Quarterly Review* 66 (October 1992): 539–45.

Schmidt, Jalane. "Women in CPS: 'Never Been Asked.' " *The Mennonite*, 23 July 1991, 307.

Schmidt, Kimberly. "The North Newton WILPF: Educating for Peace." *Mennonite Life* 40 (December 1985): 8–13.

Schott, Linda. "The Women's Peace Party and the Moral Basis for Women's Pacifism." *Frontiers* 8 (1985): 18–24.

Sherman, Gene. "Conchies Toil Unashamed." *Los Angeles Times*, 1 May 1943, sec. 1.

Sleater, Bert J. "C.O. Camp." *Peoria Journal Transcript*, 14 December 1941, editorial page.

Snyder, Arnold. "Women in the Church." *Conrad Grebel Review* 8 (Fall 1990): 235–36.

Solomon, Barbara Miller. "Dilemmas of Pacifist Women, Quakers and Others, in World Wars I and II." In *Witnesses for Change: Quaker Women Over Three Centuries*, edited by Elisabeth Potts Brown and Susan Mosher Stuard, 123–48. New Brunswick: Rutgers University Press, 1989.

Sprunger, Keith, and John D. Thiesen. "Mennonite Military Service in World War II: An Oral History Perspective." *Mennonite Quarterly Review* 66 (October 1992): 481–91.

Stacey, Judith. "The New Conservative Feminism." *Feminist Studies* 9 (Fall 1943): 559–83.

"States Threatening to Pull COs' Professional Licenses." *The Reporter for Conscience' Sake* 49 (April 1992): 1, 8.

Steinson, Barbara J. "The Mother Half of Humanity: American Women in the Peace and Preparedness Movements in World War I." In *Women, War, and Revolution*, edited by Carol R. Berkin and Clara M. Lovett, 259–81. New York: Holmes and Meier, 1980.

Straub, Eleanor F. "United States Government Policy Toward Civilian Women During World War II." *Prologue* 5 (Winter 1973): 240–54.

Suderman, David. "The Returning Civilian Public Service Man." *Mennonite Life* 1 (January 1946): 5.

Sudman, Seymour, and Graham Kalton. "New Developments in the Sampling of Special Populations." *Annual Review of Sociology* 12 (1986): 401–29.

Summerfield, Penny. "Women, War and Social Change: Women in Britain in World War II." In *Total War and Social Change*, edited by Arthur Marwick, 95–111. New York: St. Martin's Press, 1988.

Swartzendruber, Maude. "Shall I Be a Nurse?" *The Youth's Christian Companion*, 3 January 1943, 427.

Swartzentruber, Henry. "A Conscientious Objector's Second World War Diary." *Mennonite Historical Bulletin* 51 (July 1990): 1–16.

"That New Order." *Seed*, September 1942, 8.

Thiesen, John D. "Civilian Public Service: Two Case Studies." *Mennonite Life* 45 (June 1990): 4–12.

Thompson, Dorothy. "The New Woman in the New America." *Ladies Home Journal* 58 (January 1945): 6.

Thompson, Robert E. S. "Onward, Christian Soldiers!" *Saturday Evening Post*, 16 August 1941, 27, 53–55.

Toews, Paul. " 'Will a New Day Dawn from This?' Mennonite Pacifist People and the Good War." *Mennonite Life* 45 (December 1990): 16–24.

Tuttle, William M., Jr. "America's Home Front Children in World War II." In *Children in Time and Place*, edited by Glen H. Elder Jr., John Modell, and Ross D. Parke, 27–46. Cambridge: Cambridge University Press, 1993.

Van Gelder, Robert. "The Men Who Refuse to Fight." *New York Times Magazine*, 10 May 1942, 14–15.

Voth, Mathilda. "Education for C.P.S. Men." *Missionary News and Notes*, August 1948, 10.

Westbrook, Robert B. "Fighting for the American Family: Private Interests and Public Obligations in World War II." In *The Power of Culture: Critical Essays in American History*, edited by Richard Wightman Fox and T. J. Jackson Lears, 195–221. Chicago: University of Chicago Press, 1993.

——. " 'I Want a Girl, Just Like the Girl That Married Harry James': American Women and the Problem of Political Obligation in World War II." *American Quarterly* 42 (December 1990): 587–614.

Wiebe, Katie Funk. "The Militarization of Women." *The Mennonite*, 6 June 1978, 451.

Wilson, Joan Hoff. "Peace is a Woman's Job: Jeannette Rankin and American Foreign Policy: Her Lifework as a Pacifist." *Montana: The Magazine of Western History* 30 (April 1980): 38–53.

Wolf, Anna W. M. "Women and War Jobs." In *The Family in a World at War*, edited by Sidonie Matsner Gruenberg. New York: Harper, 1942.

Index

Gender and American Culture

Women Against the Good War: Conscientious Objection and Gender on the American Home Front, 1941–1947, by Rachel Waltner Goossen (1997)

Toward an Intellectual History of Women: Essays by Linda K. Kerber (1997)

Gender and Jim Crow: Women and the Politics of White Supremacy in North Carolina, 1896–1920, by Glenda Elizabeth Gilmore (1996)

Delinquent Daughters: Protecting and Policing Adolescent Female Sexuality in the United States, 1885–1920, by Mary E. Odem (1995)

U.S. History as Women's History: New Feminist Essays, edited by Linda K. Kerber, Alice Kessler-Harris, and Kathryn Kish Sklar (1995)

Common Sense and a Little Fire: Women and Working-Class Politics in the United States, 1900–1965, by Annelise Orleck (1995)

How Am I to Be Heard?: Letters of Lillian Smith, edited by Margaret Rose Gladney (1993)

Entitled to Power: Farm Women and Technology, 1913–1963, by Katherine Jellison (1993)

Revising Life: Sylvia Plath's Ariel Poems, by Susan R. Van Dyne (1993)

Made From This Earth: American Women and Nature, by Vera Norwood (1993)

Unruly Women: The Politics of Social and Sexual Control in the Old South, by Victoria E. Bynum (1992)

The Work of Self-Representation: Lyric Poetry in Colonial New England, by Ivy Schweitzer (1991)

Labor and Desire: Women's Revolutionary Fiction in Depression America, by Paula Rabinowitz (1991)

Community of Suffering and Struggle: Women, Men, and the Labor Movement in Minneapolis, 1915–1945, by Elizabeth Faue (1991)

All That Hollywood Allows: Re-reading Gender in 1950s Melodrama, by Jackie Byars (1991)

Doing Literary Business: American Women Writers in the Nineteenth Century, by Susan Coultrap-McQuin (1990)

Ladies, Women, and Wenches: Choice and Constraint in Antebellum Charleston and Boston, by Jane H. Pease and William H. Pease (1990)

The Secret Eye: The Journal of Ella Gertrude Clanton Thomas, 1848–1889, edited by Virginia Ingraham Burr, with an introduction by Nell Irvin Painter (1990)

Second Stories: The Politics of Language, Form, and Gender in Early American Fictions, by Cynthia S. Jordan (1989)

Within the Plantation Household: Black and White Women of the Old South, by Elizabeth Fox-Genovese (1988)

The Limits of Sisterhood: The Beecher Sisters on Women's Rights and Woman's Sphere, by Jeanne Boydston, Mary Kelley, and Anne Margolis (1988)